ROYAL A. CHRISTIAN

PORTER, STEWARD, CITIZEN

An African American's Memoir of World War I

ROYAL A. CHRISTIAN

EDITED BY
PELLOM McDANIELS III

OXFORD
UNIVERSITY PRESS

OXFORD
UNIVERSITY PRESS

Oxford University Press is a department of the University of Oxford. It furthers
the University's objective of excellence in research, scholarship, and education
by publishing worldwide. Oxford is a registered trade mark of Oxford University
Press in the UK and certain other countries.

Published in the United States of America by Oxford University Press
198 Madison Avenue, New York, NY 10016, United States of America.

CIP data is on file at the Library of Congress
ISBN 978-0-19-064520-5

1 3 5 7 9 8 6 4 2

Printed by Sheridan Books, Inc., United States of America

Frontispiece: Royal Augustus Christian in his army uniform.
From *Roy's Trip to the Battlefields of Europe* (1919)

For Dana Francis White (1934–2016),
mentor, colleague, friend.

CONTENTS

PREFACE

A little more than a decade ago, while still in graduate school, I started collecting materials related to the First World War (1914–1918) with the intention of accounting for the impact of the conflict in Europe on the development of black manhood and masculinity in America. My principal advisor, Rudolph P. Byrd, persuaded me to study the trickster figure "High John the Conqueror" as a mode of black masculinity grounded in African American folklore. Byrd's recognition of the importance of John to African American folk tradition lends itself to community building and intergenerational conversations about the past, present, and future. For Byrd, the mode of black masculinity demonstrated by John served as an inspiration for generations of African Americans trying to "make a way out of no way" and "hit a straight lick with a crooked stick." John was a model of resistance, resilience, and resourcefulness for black people. As a mode of black masculinity, Byrd argues that John values "motherwit, laughter, courage, hope, as well as the regenerative powers of song, love, and the spirit." Like a bluesman, he finds a way; makes a way; is the way. Through studying his efforts of self-making, John deepens our collective understanding of the redemptive value of the blues; he provides a greater appreciation for the resilience of the Pullman porter; and he puts into perspective the daily acts of resistance demonstrated by our battle-weary veterans in the struggle for civil and human rights, who continue to agitate for justice. All are invaluable resources that are capable of providing a way out of no way.

Porter, Steward, Citizen: An African American's Memoir of World War I is part of a larger project seeking to understand the impact of World War I on the construction and development of early twentieth-century forms or modes of black masculinity. For more than a decade, I have collected primary evidence related to the lives and experiences of African American soldiers serving the war effort. Specifically, I have been interested in the role played by the Services of Supply (SOS) regiments in France and the men who supported the American Expeditionary Forces (AEF) in the pursuit of victory for democracy. From books and pamphlets to photographs and ephemera, my objective has been to collect as much materials as possible in an effort to acknowledge these men and their trials both at home and abroad.

As the collection has grown and become the basis for a future exhibition titled *For Dignity and Honor: A Photographic Meditation on African American Masculinity and the Great World War,* my focus has now turned toward the centennial of the United States' participation in the so-called War for Democracy and traveling the exhibition across the United States and to the port towns in France, where the SOS regiments were stationed. More than an accounting of the numerous contributions of black soldiers who labored and fought in both America and in Europe, this collection of materials represents the evidence needed to substantiate the importance of recognizing these men serving on behalf of their country and the larger African American community at the beginning of a new epoch of world and American history.

Initially, when I became aware of the availability of Royal Augustus Christian's original memoir, *Roy's Trip to the Battlefields of Europe* (1919), I was excited at the possibility of its potential as a rare account of a battle-proven African American soldier who had the forethought to record his experiences in the war as they unfolded. I was hopeful that the volume would provide a firsthand, uncensored narrative related to the challenges of serving in the US military abroad, the success and bravery of African American soldiers under fire in France, and the revelation of Christian's determination to be seen as a man in full. But the memoir is much more than I first anticipated.

Christian's ability to negotiate within the parameters of his job, the needs of his community, and his own expectations for his life helped to shape his sense of purpose and responsibility, while simultaneously affirming his ideas and understanding of black manhood and masculinity as something different from what whites imagined or needed it to be. Royal A. Christian's record will no doubt inspire researchers to ask new questions related to the meaning of service for African Americans during the First World War and the unintended consequences of doing so.

INTRODUCTION: A QUESTION OF MANHOOD IN A TIME OF WAR

In 1914, the mobilization of the world's great powers in response to aggressions made by Germany toward Belgium and then France resulted in the transformation of Europe into a theater of war. For African Americans paying close attention to the historical moment unfolding across the Atlantic, the conflict was a potential turning point in the course of race relations domestically. At a time when Jim Crow policies regulated the movements of African Americans and tempered their interactions with whites, the law offered almost no protection against the ongoing brutalization of black people by whites. As might be expected, very few African Americans understood the implications that the European conflict would have for the course of everyday life in America. But for some 400,000 African American men and tens of thousands of African American women, the global conflict became another catalyst that held real possibilities for their futures as fully vested citizens in the country of their birth. As in previous wars in which the United States called upon its citizens of African descent, especially those who were willing to make the ultimate sacrifice, the Great War was yet another window of opportunity to claim all the rights and privileges accorded to the faithful, courageous, and above all, patriotic.

In the two decades following World War I, former African American soldiers accounted for their varied experiences in the war as they saw it, recording narratives related to their enlistment, their expectations, and their memories of their time in camp and in Europe. Bruce G. Wright, a member of the 372nd Regiment of the 93rd Division in France, recalled enlisting in the army through the Massachusetts National Guard on June 15, 1917, and the violence that his all-black company encountered at Camp Greene in Charlotte, North Carolina, when white citizens without fear of reprisal audaciously insulted and challenged the validity of black men in uniform.[1] Wright describes his trip across the Atlantic aboard the troop transport ship *Susquehanna* and the activities that occupied the soldiers from March 31, 1918, until their arrival two weeks later at St. Nazaire, France, on April 13.[2] In his memoir, Wright recognizes that the majority of the black troops stationed at St. Nazaire's Camp #1 were stevedores, members of the noncombatant Services of Supply (SOS). And while he does not elaborate on their condition to any great extent, he corroborates what historians have long recognized as the unequal numbers of African Americans drafted to serve as the needed labor in support of the American Expeditionary Forces (AEF).[3] In his memoir, Wright describes the front and how the black regiments were absorbed into the French divisions and used as "shock troops."[4] In one passage, he describes his experiences in the woods near Verdun, lamenting the death of his friends and fellow soldiers.

> We walked 3 nights as we traveled nights [and] slept days and we reach[ed] . . . camp Normandy where we made our final preparations and wrote our . . . last letters home to our folks. Entered the Verdun front lines at the point known as dead man's woods and dead girl's valley about the middle of July and lived in that living hell until late August when we were relieved by American troops. Took many prisoners here lost several men and many wounded. Cliff killed in Camp Normandy. Maceo Harris, Fisk Davidson, Curtis Wash [and] Jonie McLain wounded.[5]

He continues with a more graphic description of the hardships endured by the men, the conditions of the trenches, the rations of horsemeat, and his encounters with Senegalese and Moroccan soldiers fighting for the French. Wright's perspective on the war was similar to that of the artist Horace Pippin.

An enlisted man, Pippin joined the all-black 15th New York National Guard, which eventually became heralded in France as the 369th Regiment, the famed Harlem Hellfighters, and part of the shock troops Wright describes in his memoir. Like Wright, Pippin wrote his war experiences down in a series of unpublished notebooks in the haze of the postwar period.[6] His journals chronicle his regiment's deployment to France, the long march to the front, the cramped sleeping quarters, and the dank muddy trenches in the Champagne Sector of the county that he and the rest of the 369th occupied "twenty out of thirty days of every month."[7] He describes having to hunt German snipers and prepare for gas attacks, and the nerve-racking task of patrolling "No man's land" at night in an effort to protect the regiment's position.[8] The vivid details provided by Pippin in his notebooks are enhanced by the drawings and paintings he produced between 1931 and 1939, all of which reveal the traumas of war experienced by men in the thick of combat. In works such as *The End of the War: Starting Home* (1930), *Shell Holes and Observation Balloon, Champagne Sector* (1931), and *Dog Fight over the Trenches* (1935), the artist and former soldier provides a visual record of his memories in colors interpretive of the mood that inspired them. The grays, blacks, and reds used in the paintings are unmistakably telling of the importance of particular moments of chaos, calamity, and trauma. Even still, each is thickly wrapped with the pain and sorrow soldiers must negotiate beneath the façade of disciplined manliness and placid courage. Through his recollection of events imbedded in his mind, Pippin accounts for both the destruction of life and land he saw on the French countryside, and the conditions under which he and other members of the 93rd Division served and triumphed.

Both Wright's and Pippin's narrative accounts of their experiences in World War I are compelling and informative of the kinds of challenges African American soldiers experienced in their efforts to serve as loyal citizens of the United States during a time of war. To be sure, a number of their challenges came from white Americans at home. In Wright's journal he accounts for the contempt southern whites expressed at seeing African American men in uniform, and how his fellow soldiers responded to the challenges presented. In one passage, he describes how both black and white citizens in Charlotte, North Carolina, reacted to the relocation of his company from Camp Bartlett in Westfield, Massachusetts, to Camp Greene.

[We] were the first colored soldiers seen south of the Mason & Dixon line in full equipment since 1865. The colored people used us fine and everything went well for an hour or so. One of the crackers insulted one of our boys and the war began right then for us. We got plenty of practice for the "Boche" by fighting with the dirty crackers. The Mayor of Charlotte sent order to Captain Pryor to keep us in camp. The Capt said he saw no reason why we should be imprisoned in camp, and in his speech to us at retreat the day he got a notice he said, Boys, here's an order from the Mayor of Charlotte (he read it to us). Now say he, you see what you are up against. I'm not going to tell you to stay in camp and I'm not going to tell you to go out but if you go out be prepared for anything. . . . That night there was plenty of disturbance in the town [of] Charlotte and several crackers were bumped off. We lost no men but had some shot up so we had to carry them back to camp. Two days later we were moved out of Charlotte farther north to Camp Stuart Newport News, [Virginia].[9]

Wright's accounting of the aggressions of southern whites and the reaction of his fellow African American soldiers reflected the willingness of the men to stand their ground against challenges to their humanity and manhood. The passage also provides an image of the black soldier as a model of renewed black manhood and masculinity, capable of liberating African Americans from the weight of history. This image is further explored in Wright's passage accounting for the events unfolding before his company stormed "over the top" into no man's land on September 28, 1918, to challenge the German position. In a moment of reflection, Wright contrasted the lynchings taking place in America and the role of African American soldiers in France: "But now it was our lot and even though we heard of our own race of people being lynched every day back in the United States, we all wanted to do our best in hope that sooner it would be made easier for those at home. We kept saying to ourselves we're fighting for "democracy."[10] For Wright, even as African American soldiers gave their lives for the cause of democracy in support of the liberation of the French people from Germany's grip, his concerns were also with his people and their ongoing struggles to free themselves from the brutality of Jim Crow.

Yet even as men like Wright and Pippin served on the front lines as part of the AEF to make the world "safe for democracy," the US Army attempted to regulate the interactions between its black soldiers and the French people, especially the French women.[11] In an effort to export American racism, a confidential memo detailing how to treat black soldiers and officers was sent to the French military from the office of General John J. Pershing, the head of the AEF.[12] This communiqué was not only an attempt to maintain an American style of democracy overseas, which would essentially deny African American soldiers the same freedoms enjoyed by white American soldiers; the memo was also an attempt to pollute the minds and attitudes of the French to ensure that the returning black soldiers would continue to know their place in American society. But the French had developed an appreciation for the African American soldiers, especially those who bravely and courageously shouldered rifles and donned gas masks in their ranks and faced certain danger in the bloody conflict. To the French, African American men had proved their mettle beyond any doubt. Memoirs such as Bruce G. Wright's are invaluable evidence of the kinds of bravery and courage African American soldiers demonstrated in the service of democracy abroad, even as their efforts were being undermined by their own government as inconsequential to future race relations.

Although Wright's and Pippin's personal narratives of the war are compelling for their rich detail and analysis from individuals who participated in combat, the stories of those serving in the SOS regiments in France, whose perspective on the war was from the rear and in the margins, have not been fully recognized by historians. Compared to those serving at the front, the 160,000 African American "laborers in uniform" had a sole purpose: to ensure the Allied victory based on their ability to build bridges and rail lines, move supplies, salvage materials from the battlefields, and bury the dead.[13] The author of this book, Royal A. Christian (1875–1964), was an undrafted noncombatant African American soldier who was stationed in London and served under the command of Colonel Moorhead Cowell Kennedy, deputy director general of transportation for the AEF. His occupation as the confidential messenger during the war was unusual, yet no less significant than other thankless duties occupied by citizen-soldiers. While his memoir is a rare and unique source of information relevant to the war effort and its eventual outcome from behind closed doors, Christian's narrative is an important vehicle for understanding how some African American men defined their manhood and citizenship within the context of service to the nation in a time of war, even as their rights and access to the democratic process at home were tenuous at best. In his wartime assignment, Christian took advantage of the opportunity to maintain his long-standing relationship with Colonel Kennedy in Europe as his personal messenger, while simultaneously expanding his understanding of the world outside of Chambersburg, Pennsylvania.

For fourteen years prior to the war, Christian served as Kennedy's personal valet. The president of the Cumberland Valley Railroad (CVRR) and vice president of the Pennsylvania Railroad Company (PRRC), Moorhead C. Kennedy was one of the most powerful men in the state of Pennsylvania and maintained friendships with influential businessmen and politicians throughout the country.[14] Traveling to Europe at the behest of his employer, Christian no doubt recognized that he had little choice in the matter, especially if he wanted to retain his employment with the Kennedy family after the war. A deeper analysis of Royal A. Christian's reasons to go to Europe as a domestic servant/valet are revealing of several important aspects related to his performance of a certain kind of African American manhood and masculinity at the turn of the twentieth century. There were three reasonable explanations to why Christian chose to follow Kennedy to Europe.

First, as Kennedy's manservant, he wanted to maintain his relationship with his employer, who requested, if not expected, his presence by his side in Europe. Throughout his memoir, Christian acknowledges the amount of influence Kennedy held both inside and outside of Chambersburg, and the possibilities for his own opportunities and success based on his close association with the Kennedy family. How he came to be in the service of the Kennedys is not clear. According to the 1900 US census, Royal A. Christian was still living at home with his parents while working as a waiter.[15] By 1904, he secured a position as a porter with the CVRR, and within five years he was married and working as a janitor in the CVRR offices.[16] The change in his position and income level allowed Christian to purchase a home on West German Street in the Third Ward.[17]

The Christians' ability to enjoy the comforts of modern living, as well as their social, political, and economic standing within the Chambersburg African American community, depended upon Royal's employment with the Kennedy family. In addition, his association with the Kennedy name guaranteed some form of recognition. In other words, Christian's identity as a man, a wage earner, and community leader was connected to his ability to maintain his occupation as a domestic servant for one of the most powerful people in the state of Pennsylvania.[18]

The second reason he was willing to travel to Europe was his interest in seeing France. After Kennedy announced that he was being shipped to Europe, he asked Christian if he would like to come over if he found a place for him. His response was " 'Yes, sir.' And I at once had visions of France."[19] While Christian was accustomed to traveling both for pleasure (he and his wife Annie visited friends and family in Philadelphia, Chicago, and New York) and for business with the Kennedy family on their summer vacations to Wyoming, we never learn through the memoir if he had imagined traveling to Europe prior to the war.[20] Chances are that Christian found France appealing for the same reasons as many other Americans who admire the French as purveyors of art, romance, and cosmopolitan chic. In the final chapter of Christian's memoir, which covers the end of the war and his travels with Colonel Kennedy and Major Walter S. Franklin from Boulogne to Paris to Brest, he takes in as much of the country as he can. The usual tourist destinations—the Eiffel Tower (then relatively new), Notre Dame, and the River Seine—are among his favorite sites. He also records his encounters and interactions with people in the cities and villages. While traveling by train to Paris, Christian writes about a group of Belgian women riding in the packed train car with their "large bundles of clothing tied up in sheets and quilts."[21] Although he struggled to understand the language, he sympathized with the European people and their sorrows.

Finally, it seems that Christian identified himself as a full-fledged American, wanting nothing more than to contribute in some way to his country in a time of need. Throughout the memoir, he takes great pride in the US military and its ability to assist the French and British in beating back the Germans and "Kaiser Bill."[22] When the United States joined the fight, Christian made the critical decision to pursue a position where he could be useful to his employer and his country.[23] As a forty-three-year-old African American man, he was exempt from the draft and therefore from direct participation in the war. But at the request of Colonel Kennedy, Harry Alsinas Logue, the chief dispatcher at CVRR, escorted Christian to Washington, DC, to complete all the necessary paperwork to enlist and get shipped overseas. After approval of his paperwork by General George C. Spaulding, Christian was presented to the doctor at the Camp Lee Base Hospital, who promptly said that he could not enlist because of his age.[24] Fortunately for Christian, Kennedy had powerful friends in high places, most of whom were more than willing to pull strings to secure passage for the popular valet of Ragged Edge, the Pennsylvania estate where Kennedy had entertained business and political notables.[25]

Christian's memoir, originally titled *Roy's Trip to the Battlefields of Europe*, speaks to Christian's experiences during the war and the power relationships within the American military between black men and white men and the importance of the war in the development of the global mindset of African American soldiers deployed to Europe. It also accounts for his role as the visible, yet invisible labor serving as an informant of the inner workings of privileged white American society and the American military complex from behind closed doors. Unlike the volumes produced directly after the war by professional historians, such as Emmett J. Scott's *Official History of the American Negro in the World War* (1919), W. Allison Sweeney's *History of the American Negro in the Great World War: His Splendid Record in the Battle Zones of Europe* (1919), Kelly Miller's *History of the World War for Human Rights* (1919), and *A Pictorial History of the Negro in the Great War 1917–1918* (1919), *Roy's Trip to the Battlefields of Europe* was originally self-published, printed in Chambersburg in a small private edition.[26] Why Christian chose to publish his memoir is not clear. However, we can speculate that he shared some of his stories with family and friends, who recommended that he publish a book to share his experiences during the war.

Of the numerous memoirs, journals, and letters written by African American soldiers related to their experiences during World War I, Christian's self-conscious act of recording the historical moments unfolding around him chronicles his "adventure" in Europe, while unintentionally accounting for how race served as a barrier to some opportunities and made others accessible only to those believed qualified for service based on affiliation or racial stereotype. As a result of his position both as the trusted and reliable servant of Colonel Kennedy and as a member of a marginalized class of American citizen, Royal A. Christian became an "outsider within," who because of his invisibility was not seen as a threat to the status quo. His perspective as an African American man stationed in London, witnessing the war far from the front lines in France (though he would eventually see Paris and the western front), suggests an experience of the First World War through a kind of cultural tourism. Christian makes several observations on the various spaces, the architecture, the constructed and destructed landscapes, and the ways in which people interacted with various monuments and the displayed instruments of war.

Before the war, Royal A. Christian's life and expectations for the future had been shaped by a number of factors relative to his upbringing, the time period in which he lived, and the place where he made his home. At the turn of the twentieth century, and within the context of the ongoing battles between American industrialists and labor unions, African American men were challenged from all sides in their pursuit of work to support themselves and their families. In Pennsylvania, American-born whites and European immigrants openly contested African American men for the limited number of well-paying jobs available, especially those in the steel industry and on the railroad.[27] For African American men in Chambersburg, the world of work was in some way or another closely linked to the railroad industry. Working primarily as unskilled labor, African American men found employment as day laborers, waiters, porters, and janitors. They served as the attendants in the hotels and restaurants, and on the passenger trains on the CVRR. Because white men considered these positions fit for black men and nonthreatening to their sense of manhood, these kinds of jobs became important not only as sources of income, but foundational for economic stability, social mobility, and political activism.

In the decades prior to the First World War, African American railroad workers throughout the state were denied the protections provided by organized labor and were often used by industrialists as strikebreakers to lower the working wage.[28] The hiring of African American men, most of whom were denied membership in the various unions, not only depressed wages but served to increase the racial animosity and violence white men directed toward their black competition. In the eyes of white men, the willingness of African Americans to take the most menial jobs and work their way up to better paying positions was demoralizing and threatened their ability to find and secure work.[29] By 1914, wages for African American service workers and day laborers were low, and very few challenged their employers' policies for fear of retaliation through the loss of potential income and possible blacklisting. This would change after World War I, when labor organizer A. Philip Randolph used the momentum and confidence gained by the soldiers returning from Europe to help create the Brotherhood of Sleeping Car Porters. The organization pushed for the establishment of a fair wage for African American passenger car porters who made the Pullman luxury sleeping cars appealing to paying white consumers across the country.[30]

For a time, the war in Europe provided a boost to the local economies of northern industrial cities, as the railroads transported the materials needed to make steel to mills, which made the armaments necessary to supply the machinery for war. To meet the growing demand for labor, manufacturers began recruiting African American workers from the South. This movement of workers and their families to the northern urban industrial areas of the country initiated what is known historically as the Great Migration. From 1915 to 1925, the movement of African Americans from the rural southern regions of the United States to urban industrial cities such as Detroit, Chicago, New York, and Pittsburgh would have a lasting effect on American social, political, economic, and cultural history.

Royal A. Christian's job as a porter with the CVRR did more than pay his bills; it provided him with security, a voice, and a sense of power. The average porter earned between $50 to $100 per month in salary and tips, so Christian's income far exceeded the $6 to $14 per week earned by African American laborers.[31] Porters were well-traveled individuals who provided information about local happenings, events, and people to communities along their route. Some of the more enterprising porters delivered black newspapers like the *Chicago Defender* and the *Pittsburgh Courier* to subscribers in the small towns they passed through, becoming national representatives for the papers while earning additional income in the process. Moreover, within the African American community the occupation of train porter was recognized as a prestigious one that proved to be socially, economically, and politically important. While railroad owners capitalized on the history and fetish of black servitude to appeal to their white patrons' sense of superiority, the porter's ability to wear a mask of deference and play the role of the dutiful servant who aimed to please the white passengers assigned to his car created the necessary psychological buffer between stereotyped expectations and imagined future opportunities concealed by the act of masking.[32] Still, there can be no doubt that Christian's occupation as a porter could be difficult in terms of dealing with whites who could never imagine him as a man in full or separate the history of slavery and black servitude from his pursuit of financial gain, social mobility, and political power.

Royal A. Christian Jr. was born in Chambersburg Pennsylvania, on April 4, 1875. He would die there in 1964 at the age of eighty-nine. His parents, Mary and Royal A. Christian Sr., had been slaves in Virginia and were more than aware of the ways white folks helped to shape their son's education about the world and his place in it. Sometime between 1870 and 1875, the couple moved north to Chambersburg from their birthplace near Lynchburg. No doubt the choice was both economic and social, as the numbers of jobs in Lynchburg available for blacks were few and limited to labor-intensive positions found in the tobacco industry. At the end of the Civil War, the population of African Americans in Lynchburg began to increase significantly due to the numbers of freed people migrating into the city in search of work and the security found in urban black communities. Unfortunately, the increased population created additional competition for the already limited employment available. Like hundreds of thousands of former slaves, Royal A. Christian Sr. chose to cast his lot elsewhere as he sought to establish a better life for himself and his family.[33]

Although it was not completely free of racism, Chambersburg maintained the promise of jobs and opportunity, as well as a future for children to grow up away from the harsh existence the Christians had known in their youth. For the Christian family it represented a gateway to freedom. Less than twenty miles from the Mason-Dixon Line, this northern city had been a stronghold for abolitionists bent on freeing blacks from the institution of slavery. It was also one of the numerous destinations for enslaved African Americans traveling on the Underground Railroad. These escaped slaves stole themselves away from their owners in an effort to see the promised land of the north and a clear passage to Canada, the closest country where slavery did not exist.

Chambersburg was also the place where John Brown met his friend and fellow abolitionist Frederick Douglass in August 1859, a few weeks before Brown's organized attack on Harpers Ferry failed. Brown and his coconspirators were eventually captured and hanged for treason. The appeal of Chambersburg may have been this somewhat hallowed history of resistance and resilience that was still alive at the end of the Civil War and slavery. With this history in mind, the black community of Franklin County, Pennsylvania, had plenty to be proud of in 1878, when the city memorialized the soldiers in blue who fought for the Union cause. On July 17, more than fifteen thousand people turned out to witness the dedication ceremony of the Civil War memorial fountain, a gesture of recognition to those who fought and died to keep the Union together and to free enslaved African Americans from bondage.[34]

While Royal A. Christian Sr. used his muscle as a day laborer, Mary Christian found work as a domestic servant in the homes of white people in and around Chambersburg.[35] By 1894, the marriage produced seven children: Martha Anne Elizabeth (1873), Royal Augustus Jr. (1875), John Lindsey (1878), Blanche M. (1881), Serginia F. (1887),

Edna S. (1891), and Orvil A. (1894).[36] The Christian children would have attended primary school at the West German Street Schoolhouse for colored children,[37] and based on their passing a qualifying examination, they would have matriculated at the integrated gender-specific high schools for boys and girls.[38] Because education was so important to the African American community's development, its leadership took every opportunity to break down the barriers to getting quality facilities and teachers.

By 1895, the African American community, led by Rev. D. P. Brown of St. James African Methodist Episcopal (AME) Church and with the support of various white residents of the city, began to challenge the school board of Chambersburg and the power of the exclusively white male roster of directors to keep black children from the white primary schools. Brown argued that the board should "give the colored schools colored teachers instead of the white teachers now laboring with the colored intellects, or ... place all the colored children in white schools."[39] Clearly, there were two issues that the pastor wanted addressed. The first was the quality of the white teachers assigned to the colored schools and the need to have the resources to hire African American teachers to guide the black children academically, culturally, and socially. The second issue was the quality of schools and teaching provided to the white children of the city compared to that of the black children. For African Americans in Chambersburg, this was a clear indicator that the color line was drawn and supported by local politicians. The resulting inequities would soon lead to the separate-but-equal legislation responsible for shaping the economic power and the political future of African Americans throughout the twentieth century.

In response, African American communities took on the responsibility of educating their children by instilling a sense of racial responsibility. In essence, these communities committed themselves to teaching their children how to strive toward excellence in all things for the good of the race. The Christian family and their black neighbors developed and relied on each other to protect not only their children's physical and emotional well-being, but also their collective social, economic, and political interests as well. As charter members of St. James AME Church, Mary and Royal A. Christian Sr. made a commitment to helping their children establish a moral foundation based on the tenets of their faith. As a practice, the minister of the St. James AME gave an annual sermon on the need to "work earnestly for the moral, mental and spiritual elevation of the children, and thereby elevate the race."[40] St. James AME took an important leadership role in providing structure in the community, providing a sense of purpose and direction that allowed its children to develop race consciousness and race confidence.

This was the community in which Royal A. Christian Jr. came of age at the end of the nineteenth century, when the rights won by African Americans, an outcome of the Civil War and the adoption of the Thirteenth, Fourteenth, and Fifteenth Amendments, were threatened by whites fearful of black competition for jobs. Indeed, by the 1880s the gains slowly began to dissolve, to be replaced by a new era of racially motivated terrorism, subjugation, and government supported second-class citizenship.[41] The hard-fought rights that had allowed African Americans a window of opportunity to use their new-found citizenship were now being sacrificed in an effort to unify white people and their joint interests in regulating or denying outright the progress of African Americans. The question of what to do with the Negro once again became the subject of public and private debate. The "Negro problem" was the overriding concern for white politicians and their constituencies, especially when jobs were on the line.[42]

By the 1890s Royal A. Christian Jr. was old enough to begin to recognize the reality of a dramatically changing world filled with high hopes and limited opportunities. White men, newly arrived European immigrants, and government officials conspired to eliminate blacks from the pools of competition necessary to feed the capitalist appetite for cheap labor and high profits.[43] With the color line drawn and affirmed by *Plessy v. Ferguson* in 1896, local businessmen, city officials, and unions adopted Jim Crow policies to exclude and deny black people access to services, hotels, restaurants, and amusements they had been accustomed to visiting as patrons.[44] The color line served to prevent African Americans in general and African American men in particular from exercising their full citizenship rights, which prior to emancipation were the sole domain of white men. Therefore, American citizenship rights were inextricably linked to manhood rights, which imbued white men with power. The efforts to keep African Americans in their place through Jim Crow legislation were essentially a means by which to preserve white masculinity and manhood as the personification of American manhood. Through caricatures, blackface minstrelsy, and the disturbing act of lynching, the demonization of black men as buffoons and brutes-in-waiting perpetuated an environment in which an African American man, regardless of class, education, or religious conviction, was viewed as an enemy combatant for those white men needing to assert their claim to manhood. Such a claim would be denied by the presence of assertive, educated, and successful African American men and women. In response to the threat of competition for the benefits of social, economic, and political power, officials used the legal system to effectively criminalize blackness.

Recognizing the growing threat to white masculinity, a white Lutheran minister in Chambersburg, G. C. H. Hasskari, published *"The Missing Link"; or, The Negro's Ethnological Status* (1898), a book in which he strongly advocated for the emigration of African Americans to the continent of Africa as an answer to the race question. To further perpetuate a difference between the so-called races, Hasskari argued that blacks were not human beings, but another species of "beast" that had found its way onto Noah's ark.[45] Clearly, his views reflect a deep-seated hatred of black people.

In response to Hasskari's accusations of the racial inferiority of blacks, Reverend B. J. Bolding, the pastor of AME Zion Church, also of Chambersburg, who was educated at Howard University, Temple College, and the Divinity School of Philadelphia, published a pamphlet titled "What of the Negro Race? Bolding vs. Hasskari." In this document Bolding takes Hasskari to task, arguing that people of African descent have every right to claim citizenship in a country that they have contributed to. In his essay, Bolding writes: "I do not favor the Negro going to Africa, no more than for the Irish to go back to Ireland and the German to Germany, etc. We asked not to come here. Our labor for 250 years have tilled the soil, cleared the forest and materially assisted in advancing higher civilization."[46] Bolding continues by refuting all notions of a polygenesis, or the existence of a separate species of subhuman or beast, which Africans and their descendants were supposed to represent. He concludes by insisting that the Negro has a history older than that of European Americans, most of whom are so quick to reduce people of African descent to beasts of burden to justify the continued abuse they administer wholesale. Bolding maintained that black Americans' history could not be robbed from them by an opportunistic class of people whose sense of power was based on lies and whose morals were based on anything but the principles of Christianity. The fact remained that the Civil War and Reconstruction eroded the fantasy of white supremacy, and with each successful stride made by former slaves and their children, American society changed for the better.

This was the environment that Royal A. Christian Jr. grew up in. His membership in the AME Church, his exposure and interactions with men such as Rev. Brown and Rev. Bolding, and the commitment of the African American community to its children served as the basis for his overall education about the world, its possibilities, and its pitfalls. In addition, his penmanship, his structured style of writing, and his use of an extensive vocabulary throughout his memoir, which was exceptional, suggest that he completed high school before joining the workforce. In any event, by 1900 Christian had found work in a typical job for African American men, as a waiter and steward at the Chambersburg Elks Club. This post provided him with the financial means to marry in 1901. By 1910 Christian and his wife, Anna, were able to purchase a home on West German Street.[47]

Somewhere in that decade, Christian took a new job working for the Cumberland Valley Railroad (CVRR) as a janitor and porter. In 1904, he began working for Moorhead C. Kennedy as his personal valet.[48] While he learned how to negotiate the complexities related to life in Chambersburg as a member of the African American community, his role as manservant to the most powerful man in Franklin County connected him to the politics of race, class, and gender in ways he could have never imagined before the United States declared war on Germany.

On May 18, 1917, a little more than a month after the declaration, Congress passed the Selective Service Act. The act required men between the ages of twenty-one and thirty-one, including African American men, to register with the US government at their local recruitment stations. Some African American intellectuals and race advocates saw military service as the ultimate sacrifice and proof of one's citizenship and loyalty. But they differed on whether African Americans should demand immediate equal rights as a condition for their wartime military service. In the *Baltimore Afro-American*, which advocated the participation of black men in the war effort, the editor recognized the global conflict as the "greatest opportunity for the colored man since the Civil War."[49]

The same sentiment was echoed by the white Jewish chairman of the National Association for the Advancement of Colored People (NAACP), Joel Spingarn, who acknowledged the necessity of constantly proving the black man's value to his country. Spingarn believed that black soldiers needed black officers with unimpeachable character and moral standards who could train men not only for combat in France but also for the challenges ahead in a dramatically changing American society. However, in order to create a training camp for black officers, civil rights leaders and the black community had to put aside their demand for an end to segregation and accept separate training facilities for black soldiers. In an effort to advance his position, Spingarn stressed that "if colored men cannot be admitted to Plattsburg [New York] and similar camps give them a camp of their own."[50] Not unexpectedly, Spingarn's recommendation was rejected by some of the most vocal members of the African American community, who saw the reasoning as an affront to all right-minded race men and women.[51]

As early as 1915, W. E. B. Du Bois wrote lucidly about the impact of the war on the darker peoples of the world, and how their futures would be bound by its outcome.[52] In the *Crisis*, he used his editorial pen to demand on behalf of the American Negro the right to serve as soldiers and officers on the battlefields of Europe. He believed that during America's time of need, African Americans needed to take advantage of the opportunity to showcase not only their bravery and resolve, but through military service claim their citizenship by demonstrating their "unfaltering loyalty" to realize the "larger finer objects of this world battle."[53] Still, the threat of sending black officers to train in Jim Crow camps provoked tremendous controversy within the black community. An open letter to Woodrow Wilson from the African American journalist Kelly Miller further articulated the fundamental contradictions in having African American men fight for democracy in Europe, when at home they were subject to "cruelty and outrage on the part of [their] white fellow citizen who assumes lordship over [them]."[54]

Local draft boards denied African American men the draft exemptions typically given to fathers and men who were the sole source of income for their families. Unhealthy black men not fit for service were sent to training camps, while healthy, unattached white males stayed home as a result of the local draft boards fraudulently identifying black residents as the most qualified for service.[55] While unfortunate, this overt form of discrimination opened a floodgate of opportunities that could not have been anticipated. The fact that African American men were once again called upon to serve on behalf of the nation was significant, but it was not the motivating factor in determining the level of commitment these men would make to see the mission through. Publicly, through military service, black men could challenge and change how they viewed themselves as men and as citizens and perhaps provide new narratives for their communities to draw from in their efforts to participate in the democratic process. By the spring of 1917, scores of African American men desiring to prove themselves publicly in the theater of war volunteered for service. Those opting to volunteer recognized the potential vulnerability of being drafted for their muscle and not their minds. For some, however, that was all right. Service got them off the farm, out from between the rows of cotton, and away from the daily threat of violence that was a feature of the southern landscape. Most of these men would be responsible for unloading ships, building bridges and railroads, digging trenches and graves. Before the first training camp opened, however, African American men experienced resistance from military officials, commissioned white officers, white soldiers, and white politicians, all of whom regarded the presence of black men as unsatisfactory and a threat to tradition. President Wilson's "universal service plan" provided for the inclusion of black soldiers in the draft and subsequent military training, which included learning how to use guns to fight.[56] Members of Congress, especially representatives from the southern states, rejected the possible training of black men as soldiers out of fear that they would use their newly acquired skills to attack and kill white people.

Within the military ranks, white officers put in charge of black troops justified their use as brutes by maintaining that as either soldiers or officers black men could hardly be depended on to serve with dignity and honor because of their so-called inherent weaknesses in character, mental capacity, and moral turpitude. In a letter to General Pershing, Colonel Hershel Tupes, the commanding officer of the all-black 372nd Infantry, communicated the reasons why colored officers needed to be replaced by white ones.

> *First*: The racial distinctions which are recognized in civilian life naturally continue to be recognized in the military life and present a formidable barrier to the mutual confidence and *esprit de corps*.
>
> *Second*: With a few exceptions there is a characteristic tendency among colored officers to neglect the welfare of their men and to perform their duties in a perfunctory manner. They are lacking initiative. These defects entail a constant supervision and attention to petty details by battalion commanders and other senior officers which distract their attention from their wider duties; with harmful results.[57]

In his postwar history of African Americans serving in World War I, Emmett J. Scott observed:

> In keeping with the prevailing custom at that time of discrediting Negro officers, desperate efforts were made, it seemed, to show the unusual efficiency of Negro soldiers when led by white officers, and their inefficiency when led by officers of their own race. Negro officers were often charged with "cowardice" in spite of demonstrated valor of Negro troops in all the wars of the Republic.[58]

This entrenched attitude toward black men in uniform helped shape the experiences of all drafted and enlisted men. By adopting a policy of strict segregation to maintain and preserve discipline, the War Department attempted to prevent the problems anticipated between white soldiers, most of whom could not accept black soldiers as equals, and black soldiers, who refused to be intimidated by whites and their sense of entitlement.

As for accommodations, the conditions of the facilities for black troops were unhealthy, and, in most cases, resembled southern chain gang camps. In the South especially, black troops were denied adequate medical treatment, appropriate clothing, and housing.[59] In some instances, shelter for African American troops resembled shantytowns assembled from discarded materials.[60] Overpopulated barracks, the lack of proper sanitation facilities, and infrequent medical attention quickly advanced the spread of preventable diseases. The health, morale, and overall welfare of black troops mattered less to military officials than that of whites, since most black soldiers were destined to serve in the rear as the muscle needed to supply America's white soldiers on the field of battle with supplies, rather than as fighting as combat troops.[61]

As early as June 1917, black labor battalions, or stevedores, were responsible for loading the hulls of cargo ships with supplies bound for France, where their African American counterparts in the port cities of Brest, St. Nazaire, and Bordeaux unloaded those same ships laden with materials for the front. In France, white servicemen accustomed to exercising their assumed dominance over blacks did so with impunity. On the docks, white soldiers acted more like overseers of the labor employed to build the infrastructure and fortifications.[62] The low status of black SOS soldiers and stevedores made them vulnerable to ill treatment by military officials and the contractors in charge of coordinating their labor, most of whom asserted their sense of superiority in the belief that no black man had any rights that a white man was bound to respect. Sadly, in some instances, white soldiers and officers participated in murdering black soldiers as a form of sport when their sense of superiority was challenged by African American soldiers unwilling to acquiesce to expectations.[63]

At St. Nazaire, on December 24, 1917, Corporal William Fauntleroy, a black soldier assigned to the 804th and 801st Battalion Transportation Corps, was killed by a white guard who claimed that while transporting the corporal to the guardhouse, he tried to "make an attack on him."[64] In his sworn deposition, Sargent Willie Davis believed that the corporal was too drunk to fight or salute, the latter being the real reason why the guard shot and killed Fauntleroy. Another example of this kind of extra justice took place in Is-sur-Tille, near Dijon. Private Philip Bell testified that in late June or early July 1918, the military police arrested the unnamed black soldier and after delivering him to the guardhouse, the mob of fifteen to twenty white American soldiers dragged the unarmed black soldier to the edge of camp, where they hanged him.[65] Private Bell testified that the black soldier was lynched because he was dating a French woman. Clearly, the white American soldiers saw the French woman's choice of the black soldier over them as an affront to their manhood—but even more severely, the black soldier's pursuit of a white woman was not in line with the social contract reinforced by Jim Crow in the United States.

By October 1917, Christian's employer, M. C. Kennedy, was summoned to service by William Wallace Atterbury, the vice president of the Pennsylvania Railroad, who had been given the enormous task of organizing and operating the railway transportation system in Europe by General Pershing.[66] Commissioned as a brigadier general, Wallace wanted his most trusted advisors with him, and Kennedy was at the top of his list. This is where Christian's journal begins. At first glance, the experiences of the personal valet for Colonel Kennedy and his travels in Europe represent a minor narrative in the overall experiences of African American men during the First World War. However, his perspective adds to our collective understanding of African Americans serving during the war. His observations related to the people, places, and events in his quest to get to Kennedy in England are compelling. For example, prior to his departure for England on the transport ship *Minnekahda*, Christian records in his memoir that there are thirteen similar vessels traveling in a convoy across the Atlantic. Along with the ship packed with more than forty thousand soldiers there are thirty submarine chasers, four airships, and one cruiser assigned to protect the convoy. He provides details related to his position on the ship as a third-class steward assigned to wait tables in the officers' dining room. He also reflects on the convoy's close call with a German submarine and the relief they felt when it was reported that it had been captured.

Perhaps the lesson to be taken from the personal narrative of a professional valet who chanced to see the world outside of Chambersburg, Pennsylvania, is that African American men have always sought to create opportunities where they did not appear to exist. While the economic, social, and political conditions of the United States at the beginning of the twentieth century changed dramatically with the advent of the First World War, black manhood was still being shaped and defined by internal desires for full liberation and external forces attempting to maintain control over the black body. Individuals like Royal A. Christian Jr. represent important examples of African American men chancing to negotiate within the brutal system of racism that made them prisoners of their own bodies, unable to fully shake the barriers created to limit their ability to move in society freely. More than anything, Christian's narrative is a needed example of endurance, perseverance, and resilience to the everyday challenges faced by black men of his generation. The fact that Christian—a forty-three-year-old man with a wife, a mortgage, and adult responsibilities—was referred to as "boy" by the interim superintendent of the CVRR, Michael Lowman, a white man in an exclusive position, seems at odds with how he saw and represented himself.[67] It is a distortion of reality. But this is the result of a society grounded on the myth of white supremacy and black inferiority: white men are the only true men, and black men can never be real men. In early twentieth-century America, fifty years after the end of slavery and the beginning of Jim Crow, a majority of black men were not in the position to change the entrenched system of oppression, but as a function of survival they learned how to negotiate within everyday American life. Based on his ability to understand the landscape of his time and remain unapologetic in pursuit of opportunities to live a full life, Royal A. Christian Jr. is heroic in his own right and deserving of recognition.

NOTES

1. Bruce G. Wright, "World War I as I Saw It: The Memoir of an African American Soldier," *Massachusetts Historical Review* 9, no. 1 (Fall 2007): 144.

2. Ibid., 145. Originally named the SS *Rhein*, the German ocean liner was seized by the US government in 1914, after Germany declared war on France. In 1917, after the United States declared war on Germany, the *Rhein* and several other German ships were confiscated by government authorities as contraband of war. The US Navy overhauled the ship and repurposed it a transport vessel for American troops. Commissioned as the USS *Susquehanna*, the ship would make its maiden voyage under the US flag in September 1917.

3. Chad Williams, *Torchbearers of Democracy: African American Soldiers in the World War I Era* (Chapel Hill: University of North Carolina Press, 2010), 111.

4. Ibid., 150–59. See Williams's discussion related to how French colonial policies supported the use of African soldiers as "shock troops," but became more complicated with the inclusion of African American soldiers in the French forces.

5. Wright, "World War I as I Saw It," 157.

6. For more in-depth examination of Pippin's life see Selden Rodman, *Horace Pippin: A Negro Painter in America* (New York: Quadrangle Press, 1947); Judith E. Stein, *I Tell My Heart: The Art of Horace Pippin* (Philadelphia: Pennsylvania Academy of the Fine Arts, 1993); and Mary E. Lyons, *Starting Home: The Story of Horace Pippin, Painter* (New York: Charles Scribner's Sons, 1993).

7. Horace Pippin, "Notebook dated October 4, 1920," Horace Pippin Notebooks and Letters (Washington, DC: Archives of American Art, Smithsonian Institution), 18. Horace Pippin's notebooks account for the challenges he and his fellow African American soldiers experienced throughout the war. To illustrate his recollections, Pippin drew images to represent some of the more memorable scenes of destruction, including shells exploding on the battlefield, men in gas masks surveying barbed wire–lined trenches, and an image of a German plane being shot down by an American flyer.

8. Ibid., 38–43.

9. Wright, "World War I as I Saw It," 144. Wright's description of the confrontation between black soldiers and the white citizens of Charlotte is similar to the experiences of the New York Fifteenth Infantry Regiment at Camp Wadsworth near Spartanburg, South Carolina, and the Twenty-Fourth Infantry Regiment at Camp Logan in Houston, Texas. In each of these instances, the reality of seeing armed black men in their midst motivated white men to confront their fears of black resistance to Jim Crow.

10. Ibid., 158.

11. President Wilson's Declaration of War Message to Congress, April 2, 1917, Records of the United States Senate, Record Group 46, National Archives. In his April 2, 1917, speech to a joint session of Congress, President Woodrow Wilson asked that the nation declare war on Germany, claiming among

other things that the "present German submarine warfare against commerce is a warfare against mankind. It is a war against all nations. American ships have been sunk, American lives taken in ways which it has stirred us very deeply to learn of; but the ships and people of other neutral and friendly nations have been sunk and overwhelmed in the waters in the same way. There has been no discrimination. The challenge is to all mankind." Therefore, Wilson argued that in order for the "world to be made safe again for democracy," the United States needed to enter into the war to protect its interests and the interests of its allies.

12. W. E. B. Du Bois, *Crisis*, May 1919, 16–21.

13. Arthur E. Barbeau and Florette Henri, *The Unknown Soldiers: Black American Troops in World War I* (Philadelphia: Temple University Press, 1974), 89–110.

14. Royal A. Christian, *Roy's Trip to the Battlefields of Europe: Being the Diary of Royal A. Christian, Confidential Messenger to Colonel Moorhead C. Kennedy, Deputy Director-General of Transportation* (Chambersburg: J. R. Kerr & Brothers, 1919). Throughout Royal A. Christian Jr.'s memoir, he reflects on his employer's tremendous influence and the great appreciation he has for being in service for one of the most powerful men in the country.

15. *United States of America, Bureau of the Census. Twelfth Census of the United States,* 1900 (Washington, DC: National Archives and Records Administration, 1900), T623, 1854 rolls, Year 1900, Census Place: Chambersburg Ward 3, Franklin, Pennsylvania, Roll T623_1412, page: 23A, Enumeration District 36 (Washington, DC: Government Printing Office, 1904).

16. Paul J. Westhaeffer, *History of the Cumberland Valley Railroad, 1835–1919* (Washington, DC: National Railway Historical Society, 1979), 280; *United States of America, Bureau of the Census, Thirteenth Census of the United States, 1910* (Washington, DC: National Archives and Records Administration, 1910), Census Place: Chambersburg Ward 3, Franklin, Pennsylvania, Roll, T624_1347, page: 10A (Washington, DC: Government Printing Office, 1913).

17. *1910 United States Federal Census.*

18. Christian, *Roy's Trip to the Battlefields of Europe* 45.

19. Ibid., 44.

20. Westhaeffer, *History of the Cumberland Valley Railroad*, 280.

21. Christian, *Roy's Trip to the Battlefields of Europe*, 128.

22. Ibid., 178.

23. Ibid., 77–78.

24. Ibid., 78.

25. Westhaeffer, *History of the Cumberland Valley Railroad*, 280.

26. J. R. Kerr & Brothers of Chambersburg manufactured bookmarks, rulers, binders, and books.

27. Dennis C. Dickerson, *Out of the Crucible: Black Steelworkers in Western Pennsylvania, 1875–1980* (Albany: State University of New York Press, 1986), 7–26.

28. Herbert R. Northrup, *Organized Labor and the Negro* (New York: Harper, 1944), 48.

29. Dickerson, *Out of the Crucible*, 19–22.

30. See Beth Tompkins Bates's examination of the Pullman porter's fight for fair pay and benefits and the role of A. Philip Randolph in the development of the modern civil rights movement in *Pullman Porters and the Rise of Protest Politics in America, 1925–1945* (Chapel Hill: University of North Carolina Press, 2001).

31. Richard R. Wright Jr., "The Migration of Negroes to the North," *The Annuls of the American Academy of Political and Social Science* 27, no. 1 (January 1906): 104–5; Wright, "A Study of the Industrial Conditions of the Negro Populations on Pennsylvania and Especially of the Cities of Philadelphia and Pittsburgh," *Annual Report of the Secretary of Internal Affairs, Part III, Fortieth Report of the Bureau of Industrial Statistics, Volume XL, 1912* (Harrisburg: William Stanley Ray, State Printer, 1914), 71–74.

32. Christopher Robert Reed, *Knock at the Door of Opportunity: Black Migration to Chicago, 1900–1919* (Carbondale: Southern Illinois University, 2014), 149.

33. Edna Christian Knapper, "The Christian Family," in *Some Chambersburg Roots: A Black Perspective*, edited by Stella M. Fries, Janet Z. Gabler, and C. Bernard Ruffin (Chambersburg, PA: Stella M. Fries, 1980), 124–27.

34. The memorial also marked a point of remembrance of the burning of Chambersburg at the hands of rebel raiders seeking ransoms for the most prominent men of the town including T. B. Kennedy, the father of Christian's future employer, Moorhead C. Kennedy.

35. *United States of America, Bureau of the Census. Tenth Census of the United States, 1880.* Census Place: Chambersburg, Franklin, Pennsylvania, Roll 1132, Family History Film 1255132, page: 326C, Enumeration District 103, image 0072 (Washington, DC: Government Printing Office, 1883).

36. *United States of America, Bureau of the Census, Twelfth Census of the United States, 1900.*

37. *History of Franklin County, Pennsylvania* (Chicago: Warner, Beers, 1887), 501–2.

38. "Chambersburg: News, Notes and Personals from Our Correspondent," *State Journal* (Harrisburg, PA), October 25, 1884.

39. "Afro-American Items," *Afro-American*, August 3, 1895, 1.

40. "What They Are Doing," *State Journal* (Harrisburg, PA), May 5, 1884.

41. In 1883, the United States Supreme Court ruled that the Civil Rights Act of 1875 was unconstitutional and that blacks should not be treated as a "special favorite of the laws." In an effort to persuade the court of the miscarriage of justice allowed under their guidance, Judge John Marshall Harlan cast the lone dissenting vote.

42. On April 16, 1889, in a speech delivered to the *Bethel Literary and Historical Society*, Frederick Douglass argued that "we had fondly hoped, and had reason to hope, that when the Negro ceased to be a slave, when he ceased to

be a thing and became a man, when he ceased to be an alien and became a citizen, when the constitution of the United States ceased to be the charter of slavery and became the charter of liberty, the Negro problem was solved and settled forever." Frederick Douglass, "The Nation's Problem," in *Frederick Douglass: Selected Speeches and Writings*, ed. Philip S. Foner (Chicago: Lawrence Hill Books, 1999), 78.

43. Dickerson, *Out of the Crucible*, 15–17.

44. In 1884, an editorial in the *State Journal* stated, "And now we have for the first time in the history of our fair burg a place of amusement—a skating rink—which discriminates against colored people on account of color. They might discriminate against many who go there on account of character." The article continues by informing the reader that a petition was circulated by a handful of white men "asking the managers of the skating rink to exclude colored citizens from equal privileges." There was no response from the owner of the rink recorded in the column. "Chambersburg," *State Journal*, December 13, 1884.

45. G. C. H. Hasskari, *"The Missing Link"; or, The Negro's Ethnological Status* (Chambersburg, PA: Democratic News, 1898), 174–76.

46. B. J. Bolding, "What of the Negro Race? Bolding vs. Hasskari," *Democratic News* 4 (1898): 37.

47. *United States of America, Bureau of the Census, Thirteenth Census of the United States, 1910.*

48. Patricia Hill Collins, "Learning from the Outsider Within: The Sociological Significance of the Black Feminist Thought," *Social Problems* 33, no. 6 (1986): 14–32.

49. "War Secretary Approves Negro Officers Camp," *Afro-American*, May 19, 1917.

50. "Officers," *Crisis*, June 1917.

51. "Jim Crow Training Camps—No!," *Chicago Defender*, April 28, 1917.

52. Opinions: "The War," *Crisis*, July 1915.

53. Editorial, *Crisis*, June 1917.

54. "The Disgrace of Democracy," *Afro-American*, August 25, 1917.

55. See Barbeau and Henri, *The Unknown Soldiers*, 34–38, and Williams, *Torchbearers of Democracy*, 52–58.

56. "South Opposes Negro Soldiers," *Afro-American*, April 14, 1917, 1.

57. Emmett J. Scott, *Scott's Official History of the American Negro in the World War* (Chicago: Homewood, 1919), 431.

58. Ibid., 433.

59. Scott, *Scott's Official History*, 429.

60. Barbeau and Henri, *The Unknown Soldiers*, 51; Williams, *Torchbearers of Democracy*, 79.

61. Williams, *Torchbearers of Democracy*, 111.

62. Barbeau and Henri, *The Unknown Soldiers*, 94–95.

63. Williams, *Torchbearers of Democracy*, 113.

64. US Congress, *Alleged Executions Without Trials in France* (Washington, DC: US Government Printing Offices, 1923), 909–10.

65. Ibid., 914–20.

66. "Col. M. C. Kennedy Now on the Way Home," *Record Herald*, December 23, 1918, 1.

67. Christian, *Roy's Trip to the Battlefields of Europe*, 22.

PORTER, STEWARD, CITIZEN

CHAPTER I

Trying to Get in the Army

On Friday, October 5th, 1917, President M. C. Kennedy,[1] of the Cumberland Valley Railroad,[2] sent for me to come to his office and said, "Roy, I am going to France; I am sorry I cannot take you along but when I get over there, if I find a place for you, do you want to come?" I said, "Yes, sir." And I at once had visions of France.

On Sunday, October 7th, I went to Ragged Edge[3] to pack for him, and packed trunk and suitcases. Car 41 came out 3:55 p.m. and was put on Train No. 10 for Philadelphia. The party was Colonel M. C. Kennedy,

---

1. Moorhead Cowell (M. C.) Kennedy (1862–1936) was born in Chambersburg, Pennsylvania, to Arianna Stuart Kennedy (1836–1921) and Judge Thomas Benton (T. B.) Kennedy (1827–1905). Preceded by his father, who served as president of the Cumberland Valley Railroad from 1873–1905, Kennedy became the president of the Cumberland Valley Railroad (CVRR) in 1913 and remained until 1919. Paul J. Westhaeffer, *History of the Cumberland Valley Railroad, 1835–1919* (Washington, DC: National Railway Historical Society, 1979), 322.

2. The CVRR was originally chartered in 1831 as a major transportation line in the state of Pennsylvania. It was innovative in the creation of the passenger car, which could carry up to fourteen people per car. Westhaeffer, *History of the Cumberland Valley Railroad,* 5.

3. Built in 1912, Ragged Edge was M. C. Kennedy's nine-bedroom estate in Chambersburg. The facility was used to entertain hundreds of guests at a time. Christian was well known to the numerous politicians, businessmen, and important citizens invited to attend the festivities.

In 1904, Royal A. Christian (bottom left) and Thomas Wells (bottom right) were among the few African American men working for the Cumberland Valley Railroad. Christian's employer, Moorhead Cowell Kennedy, standing on the platform of the train, second from the left, was the president of the Cumberland Valley Railroad and vice president of the Pennsylvania Railroad Company. Courtesy of Maurice Marotte

Mrs. M. C. Kennedy,[4] Miss Margaret Kennedy,[5] and Arthur G. Houser— Mr. J. B. Hoyer, chief clerk to the president riding as far as Harrisburg. On arrival at Philadelphia the party went to the Bellevue-Stratford Hotel for the night. We left Philadelphia at 4 p.m. Monday for New York, the party going to the Waldorf for the night. As Hotel rooms were very scarce the president allowed several members that had joined the party at Philadelphia and that were going over in the same party to sleep in Car 41 at New York.

4. Margaret Coyle Kennedy (1863–1947) was born in Philadelphia, Pennsylvania, to Susan M. Coyle (1837–?) and James H. Coyle (1829–?). She and M. C. Kennedy married in 1892.
5. Margaret Kennedy (1896–?), the daughter of Margaret C. and Moorhead Kennedy, was born in Chambersburg.

At 4:30 p.m. the Boss rang for me and said "Roy, you may get the uniform out, I want to keep on these clothes as long as possible; about 5 p.m. I will change." At 5:12 p.m. he said, "Roy, we will, I guess, have to do it." Everything was ready and he donned the natty uniform. Of course, Roy had the honor—and I might say here that I am feeling shaky that if I don't soon get "over there" someone else will be getting in on me with that honor.

He was commissioned major and he sure looked good. Mrs. Kennedy said so and I know it was right cause I thought so before she saw him. I asked the boss if he wanted the stock collar or his regular collar, [and] he said, "I am not going to let them rob me of all my trimmings. I will stick to the high collar."

After taking all baggage to the Waldorf, I came back to the car and Captain Jack Study and wife, Major Carrol Bunting, Major H. C. Booz, Captain I. A. Miller, Captain C. A. Walter said they would sleep on Car 41 that night, and they did.

I went to the Waldorf Astoria Hotel at 7 a.m. on Tuesday, where I helped dress the Major for his trip across the pond. We left the hotel at 9:25 a.m. in a taxi for Pier 60, Major Kennedy, Mr. T. B. Kennedy,[6] A. G. Houser, and Roy. After standing on the pier and meeting all the other railroad men that joined the party, we walked aboard *The Baltic*[7] at 10:45 a.m. I had it in my head all along that such a thing was possible as to get into the stateroom and hide but I found when you get on the pier in these war times you do not get such a chance. The entire party told me they would have me there with them just as soon as things could get settled. So as to be ready for the call, I got vaccinated on October 26, and shot in the arm for typhoid December 17, by Dr. Gelwix,[8] the CVRR

---

6. Thomas B. Kennedy Jr. (1870–1946), the younger brother of Moorhead C. Kennedy, was born in 1870. He became one of the controlling shareholders of the Cumberland Valley Railroad during World War I.

7. Built in 1904, the RMS *Baltic* was used to transport American troops from New York to Liverpool during World War I.

8. John Montgomery Gelwix (1880–1963) was born near Chambersburg in Upper Strasburg on September 28, 1880. Gelwix graduated from Medico Chirurgical College with an MD in 1905. He was a member of the Democratic Party and the Chambersburg Lutheran Church. Gelwix worked as the physician for the Pennsylvania and Cumberland Valley Railroads beginning in 1906. On September 20, 1918, Gelwix entered the medical service of the United States military and served in France during World War I, two months before the armistice was signed.

Surgeon; and on Friday, December 21st, came the following letter dated France, December 7th, 1917:

> My Dear T. B. K.,
> I would be very glad to have Roy over here if he is willing to take the risk of the ocean voyage and the uncertainty of when he will be able to return to the States. If he still wants to come, please explain the situation to Major Charles A. McKenney,[9] sending a copy of your letter to his brother, Frederic D.,[10] so that in case the major should be out of town, Fred will know what steps are necessary.
>
> Possibly it could be arranged in one of the following ways:
>
> 1. Roy could enlist with the distinct understanding that he would be detailed to me as orderly on arrival here.
> 2. Come over on the transport direct to France in some capacity as officer's servant or waiter.
> 3. Come over as a second-class passenger on a French liner.
> 4. Come over as Arthur Houser did, that is as a field clerk.
>
> If it would expedite Roy's coming and assure him of decent accommodations, I would willingly pay his regular passage. This would of course involve obtaining a passport, which would be difficult. I would not want Roy to come if he were crowded in among a lot of colored stevedores or men of that class, I have no doubt Major McKenney can arrange it in some way when he learns how useful Roy would be to me. My present impression is the best way would be if Roy can obtain a passport and second-class passage on a French liner to come over via Bordeaux to this City. If he goes through England there will be double complications about passports and usually a good deal of trouble and delay. If he enlists there might be much delay in his getting over and he would be bound down to a definite number of years of service. As far as

---

9. Major Charles Albert McKenney (1871–1935) and Thomas B. Kennedy Jr. were classmates at Princeton University. Both graduated in 1892.
10. A powerful lawyer in Washington, DC, Frederic Duncan McKenney (1863–1949) defended railroad companies in cases argued before the United States Court of Appeals and the United States Supreme Court.

his status with the Railroad Company is concerned, he should be treated as others who have accepted Foreign Service. If he comes he should bring plenty of warm clothing. Blankets and one pair of reasonably heavy shoes. This winter climate is very trying and while not severely cold, it is at times damp and penetrating. Roy should bring enough money to land him safely in this city, but he had better not have much of value with him, due to the danger of having it lost or stolen. He should bring only hand baggage. If he is coming, the sooner the better.

If when the time comes, the matter can be expedited from over here, advise me by cable, although for many reasons it would be better if everything were arranged in Washington. You would have to furnish Roy with what money is necessary which could be adjusted later either out of his pay or by me.

Very truly yours,

(Signed)   M. C. KENNEDY.

NOTE: If Roy comes over on a French liner, I can probably arrange to have him taken into the service on arrival at my head-quarters. M. C. K.

As there was a staff meeting on Monday morning as to the merger of the CV & Martinsburg RR Co., at which Mr. T. B. Kennedy was compelled to be present, he detailed Mr. H. A. Logue,[11] signal engineer, who understands the ropes, to take me to Washington, to consult F. D. McKenney, Esq., and his brother, Major C. A. McKenney as to the proper way to get passports for Roy.

We left Chambersburg Sunday, December 23rd, Train No. 8, arrived Baltimore 8:10 p.m. As Hotel rooms are very bad in Washington, we put in the night at Baltimore, leaving Baltimore 8:20 a.m. Monday for Washington, arriving there 9:35 a.m. Went at once to Hibbs Building and waited for Mr. F. D. McKenney, who came about 10:00 a.m., and as he is well known to Mr. Logue, they at once began to size up this trip of Roy's to France, which lasted until 11:15 a.m.; then they went across the street to the director general of railroads,

11. Horace Alvin Logue (1861–1930) was the passenger trainmaster for the CVRR and was responsible for electrical signals, telegraph, and telephone services. "Personals," *Railway World*, November 9, 1906, 966.

Mr. Felton,[12] and when they returned they sent the following cable to Colonel Kennedy:

Dec. 24, 1917.

Civil list closed. Impossible secure passport. If you cable request through regular channel headquarters here will promptly enlist and forward man with orders to report to you for duty. Merry Christmas. Good luck. McKenney.

We left Washington at 3:07 p.m. home on CV No. 11, and from that day on I am dreaming of France and am studying the maps, the seaports and the country in general. On Wednesday, I get another shot in the arm from Miss Minnich under the direction of Dr. Gelwix at the Chambersburg Hospital. On Thursday, while in Philadelphia, with Mr. T. B. Kennedy, assistant to the president, I see Mrs. Atterbury[13] at the Bellevue Stratford inquiring for her bag. I saw her bag under the porter's desk and handed it to her. I knew the bag as I handled it on Car 41. I also told her I was going over to Colonel Kennedy. She said she would like to go along and that if I let her know she would get right in my pocket and I could take her over; she also said she would have things to send over to Director General Atterbury and that the office here should keep the office at Broad St. posted.

I went to see Mr. Fahnestock[14] as to whether he had heard anything of the apples sent by Mr. Davison and Mr. F. W. Hankins, and as to whether

12. Samuel Morse (S. M.) Felton Jr. (1853–1930) was appointed director general of military railroads during World War I. He was responsible for coordinating the efforts in France to maintain the constant flow of materials from the port towns to the front. Prior to the war, Felton served on several railroad boards and was president of the Chicago Great Western Railway (1909–1925).

13. Arminia Atterbury (1878–1937) was the wife of Brigadier General of Transportation William Wallace (W. W.) Atterbury (1866–1935). Brigadier General Atterbury was responsible for the construction and operation of the United States Military Railways in France. Prior to the war, W. W. Atterbury was vice president of operations of the Pennsylvania Railroad. In 1925, Atterbury was promoted to president of the Pennsylvania Railroad, a position he would hold until his death in 1935.

14. Prior to World War I, Snowden Fahnestock was a banker and financier. During the war, he served with distinction gaining recognition from the French government for his bravery and courage. He received the Croix de Guerre. Mrs. Elizabeth Berton Fahnestock, the wife of Snowden, became one of the organizers of the women's suffrage movement in 1919.

I could take apples, cocoa, and sugar,[15] as Mr. C. M. Davison heard that those articles were very much needed and he would like to send along with me anything that he thought would be of service to Colonel Kennedy and his party.

HEADQUARTERS
AMERICAN EXPEDITIONARY FORCES

Jan. 7, 1918.

Mr. Thos. B. Kennedy,
 Chambersburg, Penna., USA

Dear Tom:
General Atterbury received a cable from Major Charles A. McKenney, reading as follows:

"Civil list closed. Impossible secure passport. On receipt cabled request through official channels headquarters here will promptly enlist and forward Roy with order to report to Kennedy for duty. Merry Xmas. Good luck."

As it seems to be against the policy to apply by name for anyone from the states, General Atterbury does not feel it would be advisable to cable direct for Roy. However, I have just sent the following cable to Major McKenney, reading as follows:

"Noting cable. Suggest Roy apply to Wilgus through Felton."

Colonel W. J. Wilgus, deputy director general of transportation was to reach the states some time, during the Xmas week in order to recruit a number of railroad men for all branches of the service and I have no doubt that he could, if the circumstances were explained to him, see his way clear to include Roy in some capacity. I have sufficient confidence in the resourcefulness of Major McKenney and yourself to feel sure that you can work this out.[16]

---

15. Due in part to food rationing, apples, sugar, and chocolate were in high demand. Anything that could be sent to the soldiers in France was greatly appreciated.

16. Colonel W. J. Wilgus (1865–1949), former vice president of the New York Central, served as an officer under S. M. Felton in France. Wilgus was charged with securing enlistments of railroad men for service as officers in the railway regiments overseas. "More Railway Men for the Army," *Railway Maintenance Engineer*, April 1918, 147.

If Roy should be enlisted in any organization and come to France I am fairly well satisfied that upon his arrival here I could ask for his detail to the Transportation Department and have him sent to me for duty. However, as above stated, it might be better if it could be arranged through Colonel Wilgus to have him come over with one of the forces he is assembling. I am sure Colonel Wilgus will do everything he consistently can to oblige me in this matter.

I am

Your affectionate brother,

(Signed)   M. C. KENNEDY.

O.K.

Col. M. C. Kennedy, N. A.

Sunday, January 20th, having heard nothing from the cable they called up Mr. F. D. McKenney on the phone and asked him to have the Western Union show service of the cable, and on Thursday, the 24th, they received a letter from him as follows:

Washington, Jan. 22, 1918

T. B. Kennedy, Esquire

Office of President, Cumberland Valley RR Co., Chambersburg, Pa.

Dear Mr. Kennedy:

Replying to a telephone inquiry that I assume came from your office yesterday, I would say that on Dec. 24, 1917, I sent the following cablegram to Gen. Atterbury: E. F. M. Amexforce, London.

Brig. General W. W. Atterbury.

Please advise Kennedy civil list closed. Impossible secure passport. On receipt cabled request through official channels headquarters here will promptly enlist and forward Roy with orders to report to Kennedy for duty. Merry Christmas. Good luck. McKenney.

I am informed by the cable office here that no report having been received with regard to the above cablegram, it is assumed that same has been delivered. I did not send a cablegram direct to Colonel Kennedy, as I was advised that same might not be delivered to him and that the cablegram to General Atterbury would be more certain of delivery.

Some time since sending the above I was talking with some gentlemen of the railroad fraternity, it occurs to me it may have been

Mr. Gray of the Western Maryland, and upon my referring to the above matter he stated Roy had already gone; I therefore assumed that the matter had been settled and dismissed it from my mind.

I have, however, taken the matter up with my brother, Major McKenney, who advises me that he has received a cablegram from Colonel Kennedy stating that the cablegram from Colonel Kennedy stating that the cable-gram of the 24th untimo had not been received and asking if something could not be done.

Major McKenney is now taking the matter up with Colonel Wilgus, with a view to arranging for Roy's being sent to France, and advises me that he will communicate with me again within a day or two. In the meantime, he suggests that Roy be given all of the necessary vaccinations, so that if satisfactory arrangements are made he can leave at once.

Very truly yours,

(Signed)   F. D. McKENNEY

(Text of various official correspondence between the dates of January 25 and February 13, 1918, relative to difficulties encountered in securing Roy's enlistment, is here omitted for brevity.)

Now after this matter had been hanging fire, on Saturday, February 16th, the long-looked for message arrived saying "Send Royal Christian to see me at Washington and I will give him papers sending him to Camp Lee, Petersburg, Virginia."[17]

---

17. In Emmett J. Scott's *Official History of the American Negro in the World War*, he writes about Camp Lee and the troubles experienced by black soldiers there: "At Camp Lee there was much dissatisfaction among the colored soldiers. The reports, which came to hand, embodied the universal complaint that 'the whole atmosphere in regard to the colored soldier at Camp Lee is one, which does not inspire him to greater patriotism, but rather makes him question the sincerity of the Great War principles of America.' The efficiency of the War Department was interfered with, it was stated, because of this unwholesome atmosphere. The colored soldiers were compelled to work at menial tasks, regardless of their educational equipment or aspirations for higher duties, and discontent reigned because it was said the white soldiers were given genuine, intensive military training, while Negroes were not given enough drilling to give them the simplest rudiments of real soldier life and were not permitted to fire a gun. The statement was made that if the Negroes were allowed to be trained for combatant service, as white soldiers were, thousands would be inspired to enter the work more whole-heartedly, and the Labor Battalions would also show a larger measure of efficiency by the inculcation of a feeling that colored men were getting a

Traveling with H. A. Logue, a signal engineer employed by the Cumberland Valley Railroad, Christian visited the base hospital at Camp Lee, Virginia, when he was trying to get into the army. On Friday, September 13, 1918, the base hospital at Camp Lee reported its first cases of influenza. Over a six-week period, more than twelve thousand men contracted the virus. More than seven hundred died as a result of the flu or pneumonia, which caused respiratory distress and suffocation. Author's collection

Mr. Logue, signal engineer of the Company, was again detailed to put the job through and he said he would see that it was done right. We left Chambersburg Monday, Train No. 8, to Baltimore; put up for the night there but found it was as bad to find a hotel in Baltimore now as Washington. We found that Washington being dry now, the big people come over to Baltimore at night to have their "wet nights" and as you know how hot things are in Washington now there are a good many come over to get cooled off.[18] Mr. Logue went to five hotels before he finally was accommodated.

'square deal.' Not a few of the men asserted plainly that it was useless for colored men to try to improve themselves at Camp Lee, as white officers openly admitted to them that sergeants and an occasional sergeant-major was as high as the Negro might hope to reach, no matter what might be his intellectual attainments or executive ability." *Official History of the American Negro in the World War* (Chicago: Homewood Press, 1919), 105.

18. By 1918, the prohibition on the production, transportation, exportation, importation, sale, and consumption of alcohol was endorsed by more than half the states across the country.

We left Baltimore at 7:14 a.m. Tuesday for Washington, DC, and the pulling of wires for this trip was started in earnest. We went direct to the National Defense Building, arrived there 9:10 a.m., waited until 9:45 a.m., when in came Major McKenney. After shaking hands with Mr. Logue, he said "And is this Roy! Roy, you have caused me more trouble than all my money, but I think we will fix you up all right this time." To Mr. Logue he said, "Now let me see, what have you to do?" Mr. Logue said, "Nothing but to see this boy off. I will stay with him until I see him in uniform." "Well," said Major McKenney, "we could enlist him here but suppose you take him to Camp Lee. What time would you leave here?" "At 2:30 p.m.," said Mr. Logue. "Now, suppose you meet me at my brother F. D. McKenney's office at 1:00 p.m.; I will give you a letter myself and get a letter from colonel somebody (I could not catch the name) and you will give these letters to Colonel Spaulding[19] at Camp Lee, and I think you will have no further trouble," said the major.

We met him at 1:00 p.m. at Mr. F. D. McKenney's office and he gave the letters referred to above. As he gave the letters to Mr. Logue he said, "You will have some more trouble yet, in a peculiar way," and to me he said, "Now Roy, when you get over there—I mean if you ever get there, you tell Colonel Kennedy I am all right and that I send my kindest regards to him." I thought that sounded rather queer but thanked him, oh, very politely. You know, I was game and felt I was going through with flying colors. Mr. Logue suggested to the major in the morning, "How about having this fellow examined here—we could make that much better time by having that done." Major said, "Oh no, there is no use. He will pass." I felt good at that, too, you know.

Well, we left Washington for Camp Lee at Petersburg at 2:30 p.m., due to arrive there 5:25 p.m. We pulled out two draw-heads on the train and the air hose blew off a coach, and we arrived there at 8:15 p.m. Can you beat that for passenger service under the Government Control of Railroads? Of course leaving Washington, Roy rode in the "Jim Crow" part of the coach. I do not think at first Mr. Logue had thought it was the dope down that way, for he looked so queer when he saw I was in that part; but I had seen all along that the great part in the whole thing was my color. It not being a pleasant subject to discuss, I thought the best thing to do was to lay pat and let him discover himself—and in due time it came to him.

19. Colonel George R. Spaulding (1877–1962).

Going into Richmond, Virginia, I saw the brakeman putting so many suitcases in the toilet room and locking the door. I thought that looked funny. Finally it came to me that Virginia is dry and that the suitcases were wet. At the station in Richmond a big cop came on and began shaking suitcases for liquor. He did not bother me nor question me but he did pull off four fellows in the rear of the coach; they did have liquor in their suitcases. Well, he put them in jail—at least they did not get on the car again. When we pulled out of the station, I noticed the brakeman bring back the suitcases to the people and among them was a jug in a bag. The fellow sat it on the seat not very secure and the train gave a jerk when the air hose went off and on the floor went the jug and broke; two gallons of the precious fluid ran down the floor of the coach. Well, one could not help but laugh at the fellow's foolishness and at the same time feel sorry for him. I think I had once or so, the odor of that stuff but I cannot blame the train for parting—I think it was the strongest stuff the world over. The conductor yelled when he came in and got a whiff of it, and I am sure had the odor reached an Indian Reservation, they would all have gone on the war path.

Mr. Logue got a room at the Stratford Hotel, up the street from the station at Petersburg, and I found a little room up town near Halifax and Union Streets. I walked around a little before I turned in and I saw a car that looked like a private car by the blind, and I went after it and found it to be Mr. N. D. Maher, president N & W Railroad—his car had dead-headed from Roanoke to pick him up coming from Norfolk. So I had quite a talk with the porters until the train pulled in. I returned to where I was staying in the colored side of town, smoked a few of the N & W cigars, and turned in for the night. I had to meet Mr. Logue at 8:00 a.m. at the Stratford Hotel. He had a wonderful time getting breakfast. Baked apples were on the bill of fare. He asked for one. The waiter left and came and said, "Sorry, we have no baked apples." He then asked for an orange. She left and returned and said, "Sorry, we have no oranges." He said, "Well, give me some hot corn muffins." She left and came back and said, "The cook for cakes did not come this morning." Well, he said, "Now you just give me a breakfast and you and I will not fall out." He finally got something—some oatmeal and a few things and we met and took a taxi for Camp Lee, which is just outside of the town. The road for a part of the way was fair. We were riding in an Overland car that was not hitting properly.

HEADQUARTERS 305TH ENGINEERS
CAMP LEE, VA.

February 20, 1918.

From: Commanding Officer, 305th Engineers

To: Recruiting Officer, Base Hospital, Camp Lee, Va.

Subject: Enlistment of Royal Christian (colored).

Request that Royal Christian (Colored) forty-three years of age
be enlisted in the 511 Service Battalion.

(Sgd)   GEORGE R. SPAULDING,
Colonel of Engineers, NA

Recruiting Officer
O.K. enlist this man.
D. O. KEEFE,
Asst. Adjt.

We went at once to Colonel Spaulding, commander of the 305
Engineers Division. Mr. Logue had a talk with him. He treated him
awfully nice, signed the paper saying O.K. enlist Royal Christian in the
511 Labor Battalion, and told Mr. Logue that they would sail soon.[20] The
paper had on that Royal Christian was forty-three years of age all along
and my service record with the CVRR Company, and no objections were
raised any place among all the people we had come in contact with. He
sent a clerk with some adjutant who in turn signed O.K. enlist this man,
and everybody was going so good I thought there was plenty of time to
get the names of these people. The clerk talked smooth, told it was good
to be loyal to the USA, and I was all-proud over this stuff he was doling
out to me. He then took us to the Base Hospital. Mr. Logue was right
with me. I see them looking very strong at Mr. Logue for being with me.
Had he had hand-cuffs on me I guess it would have been all right but it
always causes some stir when white people down there in the "stix" see
a white man with a colored man.[21] The clerk from Colonel Spaulding's

20. The 511 Labor Battalion was comprised of African American draftees from
Virginia.
21. Christian is referencing the racial tension that existed between southern white
men and African American men.

office here handed us over to a clerk at the Base Hospital. He in turn took us to another building and we could not get fixed up there we were sent to the eye and ear hospital, a little further down the row. The clerk that had us in charge went into a room, came out with a doctor who looked me over while he was talking to Mr. Logue and said he was very sorry he could not examine me before 1:30 p.m. that afternoon. This was about 11:30 a.m. Mr. Logue explained the situation to him but he still hung to his story, saying that he was doing some particular work now that he could not stop. Well at that we went over to the YMCA and left our coats, as the sun was very warm, and looked at the soldiers learning how to charge with bayonets and saw them blow stumps out of the ground with powder. We looked the new theatre over. It will seat 3,500. I felt so sure I was going to be a part of the Camp Lee I did not get any cards, thought I would get them later.

We got dinner at the Hostess House, which was very reasonable and Mr. Logue there got in touch with Lieutenant J. S. Trainer on the phone.[22]

Well, at 12:45 we went to Base Hospital to be there early. A soldier came up to where Mr. Logue was sitting and he looked me in the face and said, "They ain't going to take you." I said "Why?" He said, "You are too old." I said, "How old am I?" He said "Forty-three." I said, "How did you guess it?" He said, "I was told." Mr. Logue then said to him if he was Uncle Sam he would have all that loose soil made into war gardens and make you fellows work them. The fellow did not like that so well and said he did enough work walking around the Base Hospital eight hours a day. He then walked around to me again and said, "You don't look like a pauper, you have good clothes on, you better stay out, they ain't going to take you."

The thought occurred to me the fellow wanted to tell us something but the doctor came and we went in and this is what followed:

We walked back to the door where the doctor examined the men and I sat down and waited. I was the first there. I wanted to get through with it so that Mr. Logue could go back and leave me there a full-fledged soldier in the Khaki. I was the same as a prizefighter in the pink of condition. I knew of nothing that would keep me from passing any kind of an examination and I was willing to go to it.

22. Hostess Houses, such as this one at Camp Lee, accommodated the mothers, sisters, wives, and sweethearts visiting the soldiers stationed nearby. Developed by the YWCA, Hostess Houses also provided women with opportunities to develop skills that would lead to their independence and support of women's suffrage. See Cynthia Brandimarte, "Women on the Home Front: Hostess Houses during World War I," *Winterthur Portfolio* 42, no. 4 (Winter 2008): 201–22.

The doctor came past and looked at me and said, "Come in here." Up I jumped in the room and handed him the papers that had O.K. on them and said "enlist Royal Christian (colored) in the 511 Labor Battalion. Age forty-three years."

This little doctor, only if I remember right with the commission of lieutenant, said, "I cannot enlist you." I asked for my spokesman, Mr. Logue, who was right outside the door. He came in and explained the whole thing to the doctor and do you know he would not change one particle. He said the only thing that can be done is have the adjutant general waive the age. Well Mr. Logue said, "Where is he?" The doctor said, "In Washington—I will get him on the phone." Then I think Mr. Logue commenced to tumble to it that the doctor did not want Mr. Logue to talk to the adjutant general but he wanted to talk, and I had thought that this was just about the place they intended to run Roy off the track. Then Mr. Logue said "If I take him along with me to Washington and am able to get the waiver, can he then come back here alone and will you take him?" That was all O.K.

Now the first thought in my mind was between 11:30 a.m. and 1:30 p.m. there was some wires pulled. How on earth did that soldier come up to us on the porch that had never seen us before and say he heard they was not going to take me in the service? He sure must have heard something. I felt all along my color was holding me back.

The doctor said he was very sorry to Mr. Logue. He said nothing to me. Well there, you can see Roy met his Waterloo, and you can take it from me if I ever catch up with Colonel M. C. Kennedy, he will never get 3,000 miles from me again, believe me, if he does it won't be my fault.

It was decided that Mr. Logue would call on the adjutant general at Washington the next day and that if he would waive the three years for me, Mr. Logue thought it would be best to have the doctor look me over while I was there as to whether I would pass. The doctor did not seem anxious to do so. Mr. Logue insisted and the doctor stated he would look me over. He laid me on the bed, sounded my heart, lungs, tested my eyes, cracked me on the knees, had me read letters on a black board about twenty-five feet while he held a book over the other eye, then changed to the other eye and tried the same thing, and believe me, I was passing through everything all O.K. He tapped me all over the back, took my blood pressure, said I was a pretty good chap. Stood and looked at me, then told me to open my mouth, put some sort of a stick in and there it seems he found something that he could use. He says, "You have not enough teeth." He goes and gets a book out of the table in the room and looks up something in there, comes back and goes into Roy's mouth again.

Then he went to Mr. Logue and said, "I guess I will have to reject him on account of his teeth, as you must have two molars on each side of his jaws, while he has all on one side but none on the other, so I guess I would have to reject him on that." In other words, he put that peg in, in case the adjutant general did let Mr. Logue out-talk him, he had this to hang on. Again, he said to me "You are a pretty good chap. Have you ever done any hard work?" I told him I had been steward at the Elks Club in Chambersburg for nine years and went to the CVRR from there and had been there twelve years. He said, "If you were compelled to eat hard tacks you would be short two teeth, which would hinder you somewhat." Now just think of it, me going to be an orderly and a small thing like teeth keeping me back—can you really believe that really and truly the teeth is the only thing in the way? He asked me, "Can you eat?" I said, "Yes sir, I can eat anything." Mr. Logue took the book and it was really there that one must have at least two molars on each side of his jaws. I have not changed my mind, I still feel that was the siding that I was to be run off at, I don't think for a moment every time I passed an officer he would open my mouth to see if I had enough teeth if this little enlisting officer had passed me on, and I am surely positive I could have eat my share of all the food the US has to spare and had no trouble with indigestion at that.

Well, we caught a trolley, which was the quickest way to get to Richmond at 4:30 p.m. Arrived there 5:20 p.m. and got a train out there at 6:50 p.m., arrived Washington 10:25 a.m. Mr. Logue said he would study the matter over going to Washington and then decide what he would do. He did so and he begins to see the hand writing on the wall; he seen there was a nigger in the wood pile; he got mad and said "By God, I am going to fight this to a finish." I said, "Well, Mr. Logue, I will do as you say, I will obey you; but I will say it's all up—it's my color and I cannot change it." "Well," he said, "I will make someone say no before I go back." We parted, to meet at 8:30 a.m. at the Ebbet House. I stayed at a colored hotel that tried to freeze me out. I got up and put on the knit stockings Miss Kennedy had given me saying I might need them, and they felt very good. I could not sleep for I thought of the frost that I felt sure would meet us in the morning. I felt that the train had run about long enough and all in all I felt that I was going to lose.

We met at the appointed time and went to the National Defense Building, to Major McKenney's office. Mr. Logue was standing in the door, I was on the inside. Finally up the hall came Major McKenney. I could recognize his voice. He said, "Hello, Logue." I looked out of the door. He said, "My God, are you back here again? Thought I sent you to France?" Well, Mr. Logue explained the whole situation to him and he is surely some slick and shrewd officer. Just as easy he plans his doings, nothing rattled, no fuss, everything quiet, he said. "Suppose you meet me at the Metropolitan Club at 2:00 p.m. I will see how we can outline this matter. I possibly can get him to waiver those three years for you." Well, he looked at me and laughed. "Boy, we are trying to land you with the colonel." I thanked him—I saw he was trying, too, as far as he could go.

At 2:00 p.m., we went to the Club and after waiting we met the major. He went over some more little facts I could not get then. They were minor though. The main thing was this waiver act. That was the big show. He said, he would call Mr. Logue at the Ebbet House at 3:00 or 3:30 p.m. At 3:00 p.m., I walked in the Ebbet House, stood back against the wall. In about twenty minutes, I heard a boy page "Mr. Logue, Please." I said, "There you are, Mr. Logue." He went to the phone and the major said he would not waiver the three years that it was an Act of Congress and he could not go [against] that. At the Club, I heard him say to Mr. Logue that one of the adjutants said, "What did the damned nigger say he was that old for!" Well you will see I was not so far wrong in thinking it was about time to run Roy off the track. Mr. Logue said, "Is there anything else for me to do, major?" He said, "I fear not. I have done all I can and you have done all you can. I think you had better go home and report to Thomas B. Kennedy. We cannot go any further. If they want to do anything further it would not do for either you or I to have anything in it, as we have gone the limit."

We got our baggage and started home and the curtain has closed on that part of Roy's trip to the Battle-fields of Europe.

Wash., Feb. 23, 1918

Mr. Thos. B. Kennedy,
    Acting President, CVRR Co.,
    Chambersburg, Pa.

My dear Kennedy:
It was with a great deal of regret that I saw Mr. Logue turn up from Camp Lee with Royal Christian still hanging on his coat-tails.

Curiously enough, none of us seem to have realized that Roy was beyond the age permitted by Act of Congress for enlistment.

I took the matter up with the adjutant general's office and they advise me that absolutely no waivers of the age limit had been or would be made, as they did not consider that they had authority under the law to make such waiver and, further, that in a few cases where the recruiting officer had actually taken men who stated that they were over forty, as the papers came in through the adjutant general's office, discharges for these men had been immediately issued. It is rather unfortunate that Roy seems to be so positive as to the date of his birth. If his faith were shaken in that respect, it is possible that he might get by the recruiting officer. Otherwise, I think that it would be an absolute impossibility to get him sent forward by assignment to your brother. I send you herewith certain papers pertaining to Roy, which Mr. Logue left with me by error.

I am extremely put out in not being able to accomplish the thing desired by Colonel Kennedy in this case, and if you can suggest anything further that it is possible for me to do, I shall take great pleasure in exerting every effort.

With very best regards.

Sincerely yours,

(Sgd)   C. A. McKENNEY,
Major, Engr. R. C.

CHAPTER 2

BOOKED FOR THE OTHER SIDE

JULY 17, 1918

As some who may read this book may know, Colonel M. C. Kennedy, president of the Cumberland Valley Railroad, Chambersburg went to France October 9th, 1917.

And it had always been my desire to get with him again. I was always looking for some word that he might send that would wind up in me getting to him.

About June 1st, Mrs. M. C. Kennedy in talking to me about doing some shopping for her in Philadelphia said, "Roy, you might still get over there but keep it very quiet."

And I did. About the latter part of June nothing more was heard about that, but an awful lot was heard about some changes that would be made in the management of the railroads, particularly the Cumberland Valley. I could tell by the air and attitude of some of the officials whom I had studied very well, that there was something coming off.

On June the 28th it came out that Mr. J. H. Tonge, the superintendent, would be made general superintendent, with headquarters at Hagerstown, Maryland, and that Mr. Lowman would be the superintendent, with headquarters at Chambersburg. Well that started the things to move fast. I was told by the general superintendent that there would be no porter in the superintendent office any longer and that if I wanted to be his porter on his car it would be all right, but that if I did not accept that I would have no job. I began to study the situation over and all the time praying that my kind friend, Colonel Kennedy, would soon snatch me from the condition I had found myself confronted with. I was also told that I would have to move to Hagerstown. I let that order stand a few days. I then told the general superintendent, I would *not* move to Hagerstown. I began to feel that if I had to jump off I just as well go now as later. He then in a few days told me I could go back and forth but up until this time I was still in the superintendent office in Chambersburg. The appointment was effective July 1st. On July 9th, I was ordered to go to Hagerstown to take a suitcase over to the General Superintendent J. H. Tonge and while there, his chief clerk, Mr. Andy Moore, said, "I understand your name is Roy." I said, "Yes, sir." "Well, I would like to know if I can borrow you and the cook on your car to make a trip to Cumberland with Mr. Tonge with WM Private Car 200." I said, "You will have to ask Mr. Kennedy." He said, "Get him on the phone." I did so. It was finally decided that he could have me but not Wells.

I was told to go to Cumberland with Mr. J. H. Tonge and also asked to get a cook for the trip, which I did. We left Hagerstown 12:15 p.m., arrived Cumberland 3:15 p.m. with the WM Car 200, with Mr. J. H. Tonge, the general superintendent of the Potomac Division on the throne. After arriving, I looked the whole matter over and never was there a more disappointed porter on earth than Roy. I said to myself, "God knows this ain't no place for me." I tried to play the game and get by but it was hard to do it after working for fourteen years for the real people to come down to this.

Well, the car was well-stocked and we had good meals. The officers that we had for meals spoke well of the service and that of course pleased the powers that hoped to be. Then again the persons that were entertained were not the kind that really knew, so I could not bank so much on their judgment. Well, I got by at any rate.

We laid in Cumberland until Saturday morning, when we left for Elkins, West Virginia, over the WMRR, arriving there 12:45 Noon, Saturday, July 13th. Left Elkins 6:14 a.m. Sunday, the 14th, for Hagerstown, via Cumberland, arriving Hagerstown 3:35 p.m. Went over to the CV Station and on to Chambersburg, on CV train 10, arriving there 4:35 p.m.

On arrival the general superintendent called me and said, "Now, Roy, I am going to keep you and the cook and I will pay you $80.00 per month both of you. Have the cook be very careful of his habits and I want you to go to Baltimore with *my car* and superintend the changes that I want made." We had the master mechanic, Mr. Weiseckle, and showed him all he wanted done in Cumberland. I said "Yes, sir," and was thinking "How long will it last!"

On July 4th, I had been asked to take a suitcase to Hagerstown for the general superintendent and I went over on CV Train No. 3, and came back on No. 8. The general superintendent was with me. He said to me, "Roy, you are a damn good porter and I want you. I will take care of you and treat you all right. As I said before, things will be very much changed around in the office at Chambersburg and what I fear is unless you do come, you will have no job." I began to read through the lines, but the fact that he was all the time making arrangements with Quivers to get a man and that he should take my place in the superintendent office did not agree very well with me and with the story he was trying to tell me.

The whole thing was if I refused to go with him, he was going to oust me. So I told him how glad I was that he had gotten this appointment and that there was no use in talking, he sure was going to go higher, and that I was expecting this, and that I knew he would have a car soon. I had told him that before, trying to keep peace in the family, and he sort of raised his shoulders and said, "Now, Roy, am I going at it all right?" I said, "You surely are." He said, "Tell me that again." He meant about how he was going to go higher in position. I told him all over again and he said, "Roy you stick to me." I said, "Yes, sir. I have cast my lot right with you and I am grateful how good you are." And I began to spread it in good shape and was praying for the colonel to "deliver" me.

At Cumberland, when the other superintendents came on the car and had dinner, I was saying to him, "Well, Mr. Tonge, you are like a new man. You are certainly buckling right down to it. I am surely glad to see you have the ability to handle these superintendents like you do. You are doing wonderful work." "Am I all right, boy?" he asked. "You certainly are, sir," I said. Then he said, "Tell me that again." And I went all over it. Whenever you handed him a nice line of talk he would have you tell him over often. And you know I was all the time learning just how sweet he wanted his coffee. But what is the use, you know.

I also got from Mr. Logue in New York that it was said I would not leave to go to the other side. Well, I guess they did think that but you can all see now what I had in mind; having not enough of this world's goods to retire, I just played along enough to stay on the payroll and slide at the right time—and I think I did the act pretty well.

On Tuesday, July 16, I was ordered to Hagerstown with the cook, William Howard. We went to Hagerstown on CV 5 and to Baltimore over the WM 3:32 p.m., arriving Baltimore 7:30 p.m.

I was to go to Union Bridge in the a.m. and look after the alterations that were to be made on WM Car 200. I went to Union Bridge on the first train leaving Baltimore Union Station at 8:05 a.m. arriving Union Bridge about 9:45 a.m. When I reached there, found the car, put on my overalls and a khaki shirt that I had bought for the occasion and started to work, and I judge I had worked just about thirty-five minutes when one of the shop men came to the car and said, "Is there a porter here named Roy?" I yelled, "That's me." He said, "You are wanted on the phone at once." I went to the phone and it was Mr. Hunsecker, Mr. Tonge's stenographer. He said, "Roy, your wife said you must come home at once. You must be home by night." My God wasn't that some message. I did not know at that time but since. Well, I tried to think but you can see it was a pretty hard thing to study out. I knew my wife would not call me unless something had happened and as I had only left home the day previous and all was right, I kind of thought Mr. Hoyer must of got something [wrong]. I told him it did not matter where I was, if he got word to me I would come—and I guess all in his office knew that.

Well said I, "What is the first train out of here?" The foreman of the shop was right there. He asked, "Is there anyone sick?" I said, "I don't know." I had asked Hunsecker what was the matter and he said she won't say—just said you must come home at once. Must be home by night.

I went out of the shop over to another shop where there was a pretty sensible boy clerk. Asked him about trains; he said there is no train out of here until 6:50 p.m. this evening. I said, "My God, I can't wait on that." I then asked how about trolleys, can I get one to Westminster? He said, 'No.' The best thing you can do is take an auto to Ricetown [Reisterstown], then trolley to Baltimore." It now being something after 10:00 a.m., I thought I could possibly catch CV No. 7 out of Baltimore. I said, "See what [the] auto will cost." He ran and came back in about eight minutes and said $10.00. I had just that much of the general superintendent's money. I said, "Get it." He flew after it and was only gone a short time until he came back with a new Overland Car and the chef and Roy got in and I said, "Let her go. Open her wide." And he did. Ricetown is thirty-five miles from Union Bridge and we went there in one hour and thirty-five minutes.

Got a trolley and was in Baltimore at 1:35 a.m. and took the 4:20 a.m. for home.

My wife met me at the station and gave me the proper dope [information]—that I was to go to Mr. Hoyer's house at once—that Colonel Kennedy had sent for me. Now if that ain't lifting a man out of misery then I don't know.

COPY OF WESTERN UNION CABLEGRAM
IP GY 15 PEY

London, 0035

Loco. Kennedy
Chambersburg.
British Consul New York instructed by Cable Issue
Passport Roy. Communicate Franklin.

KENNEDY.

7·35 A. 7-17-18

I had gone some but when I got that information I was really ready to go some more. I went to Mr. Hoyer's house and he took me into his dining room and we went over the situation that landed me in the care and attention of Colonel M. C. Kennedy, deputy director general of transportation, American Army. If he ever gets 3,000 miles away from me again, I will be sick or something else will have happened.

After being behind closed doors with Mr. Hoyer from 9:25 p.m. until 11:15 p.m., it was decided that I should go to New York in the morning with Mr. H. A. Logue, and we were to see Mr. P. A. S. Franklin, president of the International Mercantile Marine. I thought, well, my boss surely reached up high enough this time to land me.

I went home, packed up, met Mr. Logue as directed and away we went to New York arriving there at 2:15 p.m., July 18th we went at once to the office at 9 Broadway and was taken in hand by Mr. Franklin and his chief clerk, Mr. McGloone, who handled the matter from there. It was found that the passport that was cabled for me would have to go through Washington and that might delay some, and I feared some little technical matter might stop me. Mr. Logue said, "Why not give him something to do on the boat?" Mr. McGloone said, what can he do, and Mr. Logue said, "He can do anything." Well that caused more talk and Roy was taken before Mr. Spencer and Mr. Archer of the passenger department of the Clyde Line, then Mr. Fennett, who has the charge of

APPLICATION FOR SEAMAN'S CERTIFICATE OF AMERICAN CITIZENSHIP
(R. S. 4588.)

New York, N. Y. JUL 18 1918   191_ .

To the Collector of Customs,

    Port of New York.

Sir: I, *Royal N. Christian*   hereby apply for a
Seaman's Certificate of American Citizenship, and do solemnly swear that

(1) I was born at *Chambersburg, Pa.* on *Apl 4, 1895*
    (Birth confirmed by *Jno. Apples*   )

(2) I declared my intention to become:
        was naturalized as: a citizen of the United States on
_____ as shown by certificate No._____ issued
by the_____Court of_____at_____

(3) I am by occupation a Seaman and have been so employed since *first trip*
   last
    My present employment as such is that of *3rd C. Stewd* on board
the *S.S. Minnekahda*   en route from *N.Y.*
to *England*   as shown by papers herewith submitted.
(Seamanship confirmed by *Empft Cert S. N. Nav. Co. d. July 19, 1918*)

(4) FURTHER I DO SOLEMNLY SWEAR that I will support and defend the Constitution of the UNITED STATES against all enemies, foreign and
domestic; that I will bear true faith and allegiance to the same
and that I take this obligation freely without any mental reservation or purpose of evasion.

          Royal A. Christian

Sworn to before me this _____day of _JUL 19 1918_ 191_ .

          Reynolds
          Acting Deputy Collector.

   (over)

TAO

DESCRIPTION OF APPLICANT.

Age 43   Color of eyes Black
Height 5 — 5.   Color of Hair Black
Weight 161   Complexion Colored

Special Physical Identification Marks, If any.

_____ Slight Scar on right chest _____

Identified by signature on. Left

IDENTIFICATION.
                                              native
I _____ solemnly swear that I am a naturalized
citizen of the United States, that I reside at _____ ; that I
personally know _____ described in this application and
have so known him for a period _____ years and know him to be the
person who signed and swore to the same and know that the statements
therein are true to the best of my knowledge and belief.

                                    Address _____

Sworn to before me this _____ day of _____ 191_

                                    Acting Deputy Collector.

Address of Applicant   Applicant's Photograph, or
                                     Print of right-hand thumb.

129 Liberty St.
Chambersburg Pa.

    (over)

---

*Royal A. Christian's application for a Seaman's Certificate of American Citizenship dated
July 18, 1918. Moorhead Cowell Kennedy used his relationship with Philip Albright Small
Franklin, president of the International Mercantile Marine Lines, to secure passage for
Christian across the Atlantic. The application accounts for his employment aboard the SS*
Minnekahda *as a Third Class Steward, and the destination of the ship to England. The
photo shows a man who took pride in his appearance and understood the importance of the
photographic image as a reflection of his character.* Courtesy of the National Archives
and Records Administration, College Park, Maryland

stocking up the vessels, was called in. I was taken to the pier. I looked out and saw the ship *Grampian*, and thought for sure that was the one I was going on until Mr. Spencer said, "This boy will just fit in on steamship *Minnekahda*." That name will ever ring clear in my ears.

It was then decided that I should sail as third class steward on the ship *Minnekahda* and that I would sign up as that. Then the trouble arose as to my birth certificate. I had none with me, as we never knew one was expected. Well, it being near 5:00 p.m., I was told to get four photos of myself and we would meet at the office at 9:00 a.m., Friday. I got half dozen pictures taken, and was to meet Mr. Logue at the Imperial Hotel at 8:00 a.m., Friday morning July 20th. I was there and we went to Mr. P. A. S. Franklin's office, 9 Broadway, through the Tube [subway], arriving there 8:45 p.m. We found no clerks there yet. You know, New York clerks don't show up before 9:30 a.m. and 10:00 a.m. While waiting on a clerk, I said to Mr. Logue, "if you will get me a typewriter, I can make out the affidavit," as it was thought as I had no birth certificate an affidavit would get us through. He said all right and told Mr. Archer, who called me back in the office and said, "Go to it." I did make out the affidavit. Mr. Logue signed one saying he knew me for twenty-five years and Mr. Fennett signed the other saying he knew me for three years. Well, we took them over to the Custom House and the clerks began to ask questions. It seemed Mr. Fennett was wise to all courses to take. He bought a hand full of cigars and he just placed them at the right places. Wherever there seemed that there would be something to stumble on Mr. Fennett had it smoothed off.

I was a little worried at the Custom House; they would not allow Mr. Logue to come in. I did not like that as I wanted him to be close by me at all times. For I could feel that he was sincere. Well, they took my photos, chopped them up the way they wanted them, and there were eight clerks in all that had some part to do in making out the passport. I got through there at exactly 12:00 o'clock and Mr. Fennett, who is certainly a valuable man, as his position was important, spent the entire morning with us. "I will see you through," he said and he did. We then went to the Seaman's Home for [an] identification card. The clerks were just going out for lunch—that meant one hour wait and we wanted to catch the two o'clock train for home, as the boat was to sail Sunday.

Mr. Logue finally greased a fellow to fix us up, which was done, and then we were, we thought, through. Mr. Fennett said I would drop in here and see if the British Consul will clear the ship in port or down the river. Well, of course I knew nothing about clearing any ship. Once I was on that was all there was to it with me. Well, the British Consul was not in, so Mr. Fennett thought I would be all right. They then asked me what time I could get back from Chambersburg. I told them I would leave Chambersburg 10:25 p.m. Saturday night, arrive New York 7:15 a.m. Sunday morning, and could be at the Pier not later than 8:30 a.m. Mr. Fennett said he would meet me at the pier, and I was there.

COPY

State of New York:
County of New York:
City of New York:

Royal A. Christian (Colored) being duly sworn deposes and says that he resides in Chambersburg, Franklin Co., Pa., where he was born of American parents on April 4th, 1875.

It has been arranged for the deponent to sail as a member of the crew of a British steamer on Sunday, July 21st, and is therefore unable to procure a birth certificate from the Chambersburg, Pa., records in time to permit him to sign on the ships articles as above.

Signed ROYAL A. CHRISTIAN.

Sworn to before me
this 19th day of July, 1918.
C. Walter Smith, NY.

COPY

International Mercantile Marine Lines:

General Passenger Office,
9 Broadway, New York
July 19th, 1918.

Bearer, Royal A. Christian, is employed by us as a 3rd class Steward.

CHAPTER 3

CROSSING THE POND

I left Chambersburg on Train No. 14, Saturday night, July 19, 1918, arriving New York 7:15 a.m. Sunday, July 20th, and arrived at Pier 62 West 23rd Street at 8:30 a.m. I met Fennett at the Pier as per agreement.

He took me at once to the steamship *Minnekahda* where I met Chief Steward Mr. Sizmay, 2nd Steward Mr. Boorne, and Purser Mr. Adam Smith, who had been instructed to look out for me by Mr. McGloone, who is the secretary to Mr. P. A. S. Franklin, president of the International Mercantile Marine, of No. 9 Broadway, New York.

I was appointed bell boy. I waited tables in the dining room, and used the gong to call the soldiers for their meals. I made out reports with the typewriter designated for the stewards, placed signs on the rooms, and made a list of them for the purser. All and all, I was kept pretty busy. They always manage to find something for me to do.

I signed up and sailed as third-class steward, and in that way worked my way across the Atlantic, for which I received $25.00 for the trip.

There was a very happy lot of soldiers on board the ship, which made things lively for all.

Sunday: We steamed out of the river from pier 62 at 3:30 p.m. and sailed down the river, where we anchored for the night. I asked the gunner if there was any danger of subs in the night and was told no. I went to bed feeling contented, having spent my first day at sea.

The first day was mostly spent in assigning the rooms, getting the meal hours to suit the officers and assigning the watchmen.

A convoy of transport ships takes US troops to France in October 1918. The photograph was taken from the US destroyer Little. Courtesy of the National Archives and Records Administration, College Park, Maryland, 31019[1809V8]

It was a wonderful sight for me to look over a large ship like that. I had been on a few of the ocean liners but had only seen on the decks; but now I was privileged to go all over and I was a busy boy for a few hours.

I could still see the Statue of Liberty and even that looked good at the distance.

Monday: We pulled anchor at 9:00 a.m. and slowly moved out to sea. I noticed a great many other boats moving about, and when I was up at the pier with Mr. H. A. Logue, there were several then loading. I shortly found out that there would be several other ships in the convoy. One of the first things I wanted to know was how fast this ship could travel, and I was told it could make twenty-one knots per hour but as there were several ships in the convoy that could not make more than fourteen knots per hour that this ship would be held to that time, too.

I counted about thirty submarine chasers slipping in and around the ships and one cruiser marked C-41, and there were four airships sailing over the convoy. I now count fourteen ships in the convoy and one of the crew tells me that that is about the number we will have all the way over.

There are 3,700 soldiers on the ship I am on, and about the same number on the other ships, which makes about 40,000 or 50,000 soldiers in this convoy. Counting the crew, there are about 4,007 souls on this ship *Minnekahda.*

I find that this is a British built ship and is 700 feet long and about 65 feet wide and in port flies the British flag, but I see they have taken it down, as it is in view of the gunner and you can feel assured I had no objections to that. I see two large funnel shaped affairs on the aft of the ship and found that they are used to make smoke and are called the smoke screens used in getting away from an enemy. They put a sort of oil on the bottom of a pan and burn it. It was not needed on the trip over.

In asking how they tell the speed of a ship, the gunner showed me a long rope they had attached on the end of a wheel. This trailed in the water about 300 feet, the wheel revolving around a turn in a sort of a dial they have on the upper deck of the ship that registers the number of revolutions by which to tell the speed of the boat. There is also a wooden arrangement shaped like the front of a plow made of oak wood braced with iron or steel. Now this trails along about 500 feet long behind the starboard side of the ship and is used when it is very foggy. This trails along and makes a wide spray which the ship following will see and know how close they are on the ship ahead.

I also learned that this is the ship's third trip across, it being a new ship. I am told the submarine destroyers will go back after Monday night but the cruiser will continue with us.

By order of Mr. Franklin's office, I was to have a room alone all the way over, but it seems that James Witter and George Bryne want to bunk with me, and the second steward says all right to them if I am satisfied, so I was pleased to have them, and they proved very good mates. I being a member of the crew now we all sleep in the "Gloryhold," that is what it is called and it is the lower deck under the rear end of the ship. They are regular seamen and Witter was on the *Titanic* and Bryne was in the Halifax trouble and they had plenty to tell me of the sea, as both had been going to sea for twenty-five years.

So Monday night I went to bed about 11:30 p.m., thinking I had about all the dope I could remember for the first full day at sea and was not long in sleeping, being told no submarines come in close to shore and that we were safe until near the coast of Ireland. I believed all that.

When at exactly 3:05 a.m., Tuesday, July 22nd, Mr. Earney went through the ship saying "Everybody on deck. Submarine sighted.

Submarine, submarine." Needless to tell you I was dressed in record time and on deck with my life preserver on. I have at many times dressed fast to catch trains but never as fast as that time.

I ran up on deck and went to the port side of the ship and some of the soldiers, as a great many of them slept on deck said, "Here he is." And over to the starboard side I went, and the sub was passing alongside the boat. It happened this way. The submarine came up just in front of the ship *Minnekahda* and the gunner in the forward deck put a depth charge after it at once but missed it and a man came up and said "My God, don't shoot on an American submarine." The forward gunner wired the gunner on the rear, who had his gun trained right on the sub, not to shoot. The man on the submarine also asked, "What is the name of this boat," but no one would call the name. They then shot off three green lights and submerged. It all happened in a few minutes but the fright remained a long, long time, and it was the main topic during the remainder of the trip.

All that came on deck remained there until daylight. I was very much surprised that a great many soldiers only swore and would not come from their hammocks.

Tuesday: The chief talk of the day was the submarine. It was talked about everywhere, as to what it looked like and was it a real American sub or a German submarine. The thought of the two men in my room was that the gunner should have made them heave to and put out a crew to examine them as to who they were, which later turned out to be true.

I was told to go through the boat and count the number of fire Queens and fire hoses and report to the chief steward. On doing this, I looked very carefully at the watertight doors and compartments that I had read so much about. There was about seventy-two fire Queens and forty-eight reels of fire hose, and from what I saw of the watertight compartments they may do some good.

In making my report to the chief steward, I overheard an officer say it was a German sub all right and that it may give us more trouble. That was all I could catch there. I was very much worried for some time, thinking it might come around that night.

Well, things sort of quieted down a bit and I made up my mind that there would be no more sleep or rather taking clothes off for me until I got on the other side.

The soldiers all wear life preservers all the time and take them into the dining room with them. They have very good meals. They have seven tables in the dining salon, each seating fourteen: each table having two waiters to serve. There were 160 officers on the boat and they had two sittings. The officers all eat in the dining salon and the soldiers eat from their mess. They all had plenty, sometimes they would bring their food up on deck and would sit on deck and eat, and at other times they would remain below.

The sea was very smooth and plenty of sea grass to be seen. They say when you see the sea grass you are in the gulf-stream. That may be, but at that you have a long look for land, as I found out.

Wednesday: I had attempted to keep a diary on the boat, but was cautioned by Witter that the skipper would not allow that, that if we were taken over by a sub it would give valuable information to the enemy. I had thought that and was trying to keep from being seen, but he was in and out so much and seen me writing, that is why he spoke. I will leave it to you if you think I missed very much. When George Bryne came into the room this morning he said to me, "Roy, that was a German submarine and they have caught him." He said they had three American prisoners on it and they made them at the point of a gun say, "Don't shoot on an American submarine." The ships wired back after the sub had passed and it was picked up and they went after them and got them.

My heart beat a little easier for a while but I thought there was more than one in that large body of water. We received wireless every day from the Eiffel Tower, France, giving baseball scores and telling of the advance the Allies were making, and the stock market.

Thursday was a dry day, not much excitement. I went down and had a talk with the fireman. I asked him about how much coal it took to drive a ship across and he said about five hundred tons. The ships only made about fourteen knots per hour and ran a zig-zag course the whole way, which made the trip about five hundred miles longer. But they claim it is much harder for a sub to hit a ship when they run that way.

They began examining the soldiers and watching their condition. They found that several had a breaking out. They were isolated to themselves to see what it would turn out to be. It did turn out to be measles and after several days the doctors had that under control. I did not bother that part of the ship while they were there. The doctors also found many of the men had "cooties" in various forms. And they gave them the attention that was needed. The soldiers shoot a good deal of "craps" but the officers after several days stopped them from gambling—that is, when they saw it. Of course you know the officers did not see all that went on with that many men on board.

The weather again today was fine, the sea very smooth. I had expected to get a little seasick, but as yet I have had no trouble along that line, but I have seen a good many of them in a bad way.

Friday: The weather today was cold and rainy and not much to see. The wireless message this morning tells us of the sinking of the large ship *Justicia* off the coast of Ireland, and of course everybody is sorry to hear that and at the same time wondering how we will pass that place that has caused so much trouble.

We also pass a ship going toward New York. It was the first ship we had seen since leaving New York. I found out the *Minnekahda* is the flag-ship of this convoy—that is, all other ships take orders from her. She was in the lead nearly the whole way over and I often noticed one of the sailors coming out of the upper deck and with two flags of various colors he would signal to the other ships, and shortly they would run up a string of flags.

I often watched the watchman come down from the crow's nest and saw the relief man go up. He is up so high you can hardly see him when he sits in his sort of a basket arrangement.

Major Edwin O. Baker was the commanding officer on the ship. In the evening the officers would have some talent from among the soldiers come into the smoking room and sing or recite and spend the evenings that way. They also had boxing matches very often on deck, and they had some pretty fair scrappers in the bunch. They made a ring and made up a purse of a few dollars and they would scrap to beat the band.

I was anxious to see the minesweepers on a ship, so one of the sailors on the forward deck showed them to me one day. I thought I could get a [post]card to show them, as I do not feel that I can describe them that one can understand, but as yet have not been able to find such a card.

Saturday: This was another cold, rainy day—makes one feel bad. In talking to the gunner on the aft of the ship he asked me what I thought. I told him I thought the captain or whoever had the compass must of lost his course, as it was too cold for this time of the year. He said we will be all right after a while. To which I replied, "Brother, I hope you are right."

About 11:00 a.m., Captain Gates came into the purser's office and began talking to Mr. Sizmay about putting a cover over the stairs leading from the dining salon up on deck. There was too much light showing out at night. All parts of the vessel are closed up at night. It was also my duty to close all port-holes in the dining salon just before dark after the captain explained this. I was on duty as bell boy. He said to me, "Well, my boy, how are you standing the trip?" I said, "Very well, sir," and he said, "I hear you are going over to polish Mr. Franklin's shoes." I said, "Yes, sir." "Now let me see," he said, "what is his title now—captain ain't it?" I said, "Yes, sir." "Well," he said, "I want you to take good care of him and have his shoes shining so that everyone can see their faces in them." I said, "Yes, sir." Then he said, "You are certainly going over in great style. You are the only passenger I have on this whole ship." "Well, sir," says I, "I thank you sir. I hope you will be successful in landing this one passenger safely." He laughed aloud and said, "Now don't you worry, my boy. I will hand you safely to the captain. Just you stick to the ship."

When the officers saw and heard him talking to me they did wonder. It seemed that all along it was a kind of mystery of my being on the ship. The commanding officer, Major Baker, asked me one day where I was going and whether I was going over for a valet. I always changed the conversation by asking them something. I never told anyone what my errand was.

I also said to the captain, when he said it was a little cool, "I think we must be near Greenland's icy mountains by the way it feels." He said [we] changed course.

In a talk with the baker about how much bread they bake in a day, he said they bake 3,800 loaves a day and between 600 and 700 rolls. He could not guess how many barrels of flour that takes. The bread was very good. In fact, all meals were good. I think the salt air has a good deal to do with a fellow's appetite. Really, I was hungry for every meal and I surely did get plenty to eat the whole way over. I was treated very nicely by the entire crew—a few cigarettes and a cigar once in a while helps to cement everything all right.

Sunday: The ships in this convoy are: the *Minnekahda*, *Grampian*, *Philadelphia*, *New York*, *Carmania*, *Corinthic*, *Encous*, *Canopic*, *Orca*, *Franconia*, *Amazon*, and *Merian*. There were two others but I was unable to get the names. You know, fourteen ships as large as these, keeping from fifty to three hundred and four hundred feet apart cover a whole lot of ground.

There were several YMCA workers aboard and this day they held services on deck. There was a Catholic priest and a Dr. Dreaver and Dr. Clark. Dr. Dreaver preached from some place in Luke telling the boys to have their hearts right with God, and then when you are called to go across *No Man's Land* there will be no fear, and when you write your mother don't tell her that you have no good things to eat. Tell her only what will make her feel good. Try to make her happy and don't tell her you have to sleep out on deck that would worry her.

Now it happened that the three ministers above named were among the other soldiers chosen to censor the mail on board that it could be mailed on arrival at Liverpool. When one of the preachers was reading through a letter, who happened to be from one of the soldiers that was on board from his church, he was telling his mother this:

Dear Mother: We had services on the deck this morning and Rev. Dreaver preached, and he said that we were not to tell you all that we had to eat, but only tell you the good things. Now, mother, I have never lied to you and I'll be darned if I am going to let Dr. Dreaver tell me how to start now.

Every night about 11:00 p.m. or 12:00 a.m. some of the officers would come into the kitchen and get sandwiches and coffee. They always paid Witter for it. I don't know how the managers of the boat came out but he made quite a few dollars every night. Well, the preacher was in the party one night and told this story. He said he knew the fellow had no idea that she would never see the letter. It was very amusing and the reverend took it good natured, too. They sang a very appropriate piece, "Jesus, Savior, Pilot Me." I thought that was pretty good. In the evening they sang "Brighten the Corner Where You Are." There was always a great many who attended the services and the singing was very good.

Monday, July the 29th, we had boat muster—that is, at a certain time a bell is rang and everybody must march to their life boat and remain there until told to leave. Must have your life preserver on. The roll is called and anyone being absent is fined five shillings. Well, I was there. My ticket called for life-boat No. 7. I have not much to say about this life-boat business. I am very glad nothing happened. It is more good luck than good management.

Tuesday: It was thought we would dock on Thursday but they claimed the zig-zag course had knocked us out so much that we would not get in until possibly Saturday. It was very foggy that night and the *Carmania* came near bumping into us. The vessels all had their fog signals out but the *Carmania* was close up on the side of the *Minnekahda*. The fog signal blowed again. And several of the officers that were sitting on the deck jumped up thinking it was a signal for a submarine, knocked down a doctor and two soldiers running into the boat to get his suitcase, said he had some important papers in them. Then they tell you if anything would happen they would all go off quietly—well that little dentist ran like a crazy man.

I looked now for the submarine destroyers all day, but nothing showed up. It is said they will meet us in the morning.

Wednesday: The crew was called every morning at 5:00 a.m. and we all went to the dining salon and the second steward would get there about 5:30 a.m. and call the roll, everybody answering to their name being called. Next in order was a strong cup of tea. Well, you never saw such people about that tea business. So when we got up this morning the cruiser was still with us, but we saw something away back smoking like everything, and some said it was the chasers coming after us, that they had lost us. Well, we watched them closely. Finally, they caught up to us about 9:00 a.m. and there were four submarine chasers and the cruiser at once turned back. Well that is a great game, this submarine game. I mean, they are in and out all around. And they stayed with us the whole way. Everybody began to feel better over the chances of getting into port safe.

Someone died on the *Encous* and the flags were half-masted on all vessels. The soldiers were eating some cheese that they said was bad, so they took it and wrapped it carefully, carried it all around the deck and sang "Nearer My God to Thee" and buried it at sea. All had their hats off. It was a pretty little stunt they pulled off.

Thursday: Today we find six more submarine chasers corning up to our convoy, and we sail along at a good rate, everything is going fine and we are all hoping for the best.

Looking miles ahead of us, you could see something that looked like a ship. After a while it got closer and I saw the chaser going that way. After the entire convoy got way past the chaser, it started out after this vessel. Well, it can make fifty miles per hour and that fellow simply flew. It was not long until it pulled up by the ship's side. The chasers have to be very careful as some of these ships carry petroleum for the submarines. You see the submarines cannot carry a very large amount of petroleum and they have these vessels meet them away out in the ocean. It was pretty far away but the gunner said they would put a crew on the boat and look at the captain's papers, and if they were all right they would leave her alone. Evidently they were all right as the little fellows came back soon. There was no further trouble for the day or night.

Friday: As we looked out over the sea, looking to see what if anything could be seen. There was nothing doing then. It was about 5:15 a.m. and the submarine chasers and destroyers were in the lead and away over to the starboard side.

The *Minnekahda* was leading the group of vessels, the *Carmania* was on the starboard side of our ship, and the *Philadelphia* was on the outer side of the *Carmania*. They remained in that formation until about 9:30 a.m. when the *Grampian* came in between the *Carmania* and our ship, and that way they remained.

The destroyers were away over to the right and about 10:30 a.m., we see the destroyers going with full steam ahead simply flying. There were also two observation balloons up over near where the destroyers were. The gunners had told us that this was the coast of Ireland and that it was necessary to be very careful. Every gunner was on the job, ready to go to it. Next thing we heard several depth charges. They go off like a well-muzzled blast. We heard about ten in very quick time. Finally we can just barely see something going up in the air. The destroyers then came back to the convoy with a stream of flags flying from their masts. The gunner says that means they got her. The ship *Grampian* also took a shot at the submarine but missed. And a soldier fell overboard when the *Grampian* shot. He was leaning out over the rails. They did not stop for him. Possibly one of the ships on the rear got him.

There is no explaining to anybody how the fever is when anything is going on. Everybody is strung up to the last minute and you simply cannot explain.

They tell me about seeing a periscope in the water at night. You can look until your eyes get sore. If you don't see the submarine before you see the periscope, he has pretty near got you.

In talking with the captain later he said we had taken the northern route and were near the Hebrides Islands and we would then go south through the Irish Sea.

At 12:40 p.m., we see the hills of Scotland and the soldiers simply scream at the sight of land. We came through the North Channel then the Irish Sea, passing near the Isle of Man.

The Irish Sea is certainly one still body of water. You seem to simply glide over it. You put your watch ahead from New York to London from fifteen minutes to one hour and fifty-five minutes, and when you arrive [in] London you are five hours ahead of American time.

After coming through the Irish Sea, we hit the Mersey River too late to make the tide and had to lay out all night. It is against the rule in wartime to lay still with a vessel; we had to keep moving around. We had hoped to dock about 8:00 p.m. Well, after moving around all night, we started in in the morning, and as we did, we hit a sandbar.

Saturday: The other ships went on into dock while we waited until the tide at 8:30 a.m. floated us off. Then we went into dock at Liverpool, arriving there at 9:30 a.m. Saturday morning, August 3rd, 1918.

The sight that we met there at the dock was the most wonderful I ever saw. Such a mass of people. It was really great. The band was playing "God Save the King" and that made us feel "My Country 'tis of Thee," "We won't come back till it's over, over there," and "Star Spangled Banner." Oh, it was fine. The boys on deck were singing and I mean things were just right.

All the soldiers were called up at 3:00 a.m. Saturday morning and marched on deck, and they stayed there until daylight for fear that something might happen.

I had been well posted by Mr. T. B. Kennedy and Mr. J. B. Hoyer not to leave the boat until I had signed off and was duly paid. I was sure that something might happen that they might want to hold me for a day or two after arriving, but I intended to carry out my instructions, but I felt it all through my bones that there would be some word for Roy when he arrived at Liverpool. When we docked the headwaiter said, "Now boys, we will gather up all the linen, silver and china and pack away." That is the way they do and the things are not gotten out until the ship puts out to sea again. You see it takes about a week to unload a vessel this size.

I was helping them and I stayed close to a porthole, they act as windows. I began helping to pack and every few minutes I would go up on the table and take a peep out the porthole. The mass of people outside made it very difficult to find anybody. But I thought I could pick out Colonel Kennedy or his secretary, A. G. Houser. Finally about 10:25 a.m., I saw two fine, tall gentlemen with canes walking toward the ship and "Willis," who had charge of the smoking room, was at the gangplank and was looking around. They said something to him and he turned around quickly and they headed for the ship. I thought by their movements that they must be way up. I did not know how to tell who was an officer or his rank. So, in they came and went up to the purser's office. I was nearby and I heard them say something about Roy. Well, that was a happy moment for me. I was standing just inside the dining salon door very handy, and Mr. Boone said, "Yes, he is here all right," and they called me. Of course, you know I was not long in getting to them. It was Captain W. S. Franklin,[1] who until the war was assistant general freight agent of the PRR at Philadelphia, and Captain F. C. Covell, of the English Army. They shook hands with me and asked me how I stood the trip.

He said, "Roy, we will take you right along with us now." I said, "Yes, sir." I never thought about any money. I had already brought my suitcase and had it hid under the dining room table and was ready in record time to go.

After it was seen that we could not dock until Saturday, I was told that I could not sign off until Tuesday. That Monday it was a bank holiday in England and that meant I would have to stay aboard the ship on that account. I said, "All right." But I really meant I came very close to being back with Colonel Kennedy. And I thought he would send word for me before Tuesday. But I said nothing of that to them. It was this way. Colonel Kennedy was on an inspection of docks all through England and he put it in the hands of these two captains, who are on his staff to pull the trick. Well, they surely did pull it. Why, when Captain Franklin spoke on that ship *silence reigned Supreme.* He and Captain Covell could have taken the blooming ship and nothing would have been said.

Captain W. S. Franklin is a brother to Mr. P. A. S. Franklin, president of the International Mercantile Marine of No. 9 Broadway, New York, and everybody knows what the PRR officers can do and Captain F. C. Covell knows England like a book, so there was nothing to it.

Captain Franklin told me how to go to the Custom House and register, and then to the police station and register. I won't say how much red tape I had to go through. The thing is to do it. I did it. He also told me to meet him at the North-Western Hotel at 4:00 p.m. I was there at 3:15 p.m. When Captain Franklin came, he told me we would

---

1. Walter Sidmonds (W. S.) Franklin Jr. (1884–1972) was a graduate of Harvard University and member of the railroad fraternity. Beginning in 1906, he worked for the Pennsylvania Railroad (PRR) as a platform clerk and by 1918 was the assistant general freight agent. After the war, he would continue with the PRR and rose through the ranks to become president in 1948, a position he held for six years.

go to London on the 5:20 p.m. train. We arrived at 10:45 p.m., Mr. A. G. Houser met us with a chauffeur and auto. After taking Captain Franklin home, he took me to the office where I met Sergeant Warren Smith, who is the assistant in the office. They whirled me to the room they had for me and after a little talk, I, good and tired, turned in for the night, sure of one thing—that no sub would get me that night.

CHAPTER 4

LONDON AS I SAW
IT DURING THE WAR

I got up at 7:00 a.m., had breakfast, and was at the office at 9:30 a.m. Mr. Houser and Sergeant Smith began breaking me into my duties.

Colonel M. C. Kennedy is expected back at 7:00 p.m. and I am to go to the house to see him. We work pretty near the whole day and in the evening. Mr. Houser takes me through Hyde Park to the house where I see the "Boss" and he never looked better to me than he did this time. Houser remains a while, then he goes and the Boss and I talk for some time.

Monday morning, I started on my job as the confidential messenger of M. C. Kennedy stationed at American Army Headquarters, Belgrave Mansions Hotel, London, England. As you can see, that is some title.

The Hyde Park area is 361 acres. It is joined on the west by Kensington Gardens, which contains 275 acres. The two together forming London's finest "lung." From Park Lane to Kensington Garden is about one-half mile. From Marble Arch to Hyde Park corner is one mile. It was once the Abbey of Westminster. It was converted into a deer park and under the Stuarts was used for horse racing. King William and Queen Anne caused a number of improvements to be made. But it is to Queen Caroline, the consort of George II, that we owe its most attractive feature, the serpentine, an artificial sheet of water stretching from Lancaster Gate to the dell opposite Albert Gate.

The Marble Arch at the northeast corner of the park was intended by George IV to form the portal of Buckingham Palace. It cost 80,000

Colonel Moorhead C. Kennedy, officer in charge of railway transportation, in his AEF office in London in October 1918. Kennedy took to his wartime post with the same business efficiency he deployed as the president of the Cumberland Valley Railroad. Courtesy of the National Archives and Record Administration, College Park, Maryland, 33771[2017V8]

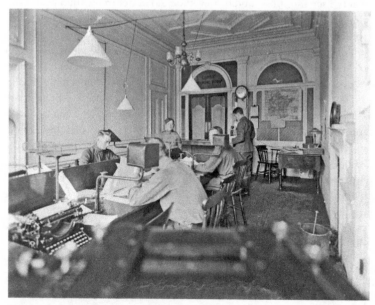

Soldiers receive and send messages in the telegraph office set up at the Belgrave Mansions Hotel in London, which is where Colonel Kennedy worked. Courtesy of the National Archives and Record Administration, College Park, Maryland, 25342[10969T8]

pounds and the gates 3,000 pounds. The Marble Arch stands directly in front of Great Cumberland Place and No. 14 Great Cumberland Place is the home of Colonel M. C. Kennedy, Captain W. S. Franklin, Naval Constructor [L. B.] McBride, and Paymaster J. S. Higgins.

There are large gatherings in Hyde Park every evening and you can hear all kinds of religion discussed, and they always wind up by singing many of the old familiar hymns heard in the States. The singing is perfectly lovely. There are five hundred to one thousand in the crowd singing.

Now, there are thousands of benches and chairs all through Hyde Park and there is a man going through the park that collects one pence from you. But most of the young ladies with their soldier boys prefer sitting on the grass, and as for kissing that is common. They have several women police that patrol the park at nights. Well, I have never seen them arrest anybody yet. They possibly don't see very well. I saw some queer things in different parts of this world, but Hyde Park has got it on all places I ever saw.

Some people might think London a great place for style. I have noticed the dress of women and men. To me it seems that the ladies here don't seem to get the hang and they do not have the get-up that the American women have. Mr. Smith and Houser were talking that over in the office when I spoke of it. They say it is true. The English women seem to be lacking of something. But sure no gentleman would care to see the ladies with any less clothes on than they wear on the streets now, and no thinner.

You can see the searchlights looking for the air raiders nearly every night and always on Saturday nights. But it seems that they are keeping Old Fritz so busy now that he cannot get over this way. The tops of the houses are nearly all painted green, making them look like grass.

Soldiers who have been wounded are allowed to walk around the city. They all wear a light blue sort of a flannel suit, but are allowed to have no intoxicants. One told me it did not matter as the pep is all out of the booze anyhow.

This is one city that you are never safe [in] without a raincoat. I have never seen it rain as quick and as fast and hard.

The streets are all very wide and paved with wooden blocks, and the driveways could not be kept in any better shape. Some citizens of Chambersburg wanted them to pave the city with wooden blocks, but they would not have it that way. One of the troubles with Chambersburg is they always elect two or three good wide-awake councilmen, then they put in six or seven that have never been any farther than Hagerstown Fair, and the progressive ones are out-voted when it comes to progressive improvements.

It has always been the rule with Colonel Kennedy to smoke two cigarettes a year; but I note that he has increased that a little since coming on this side. I saw him and Colonel Byllesby both smoking today going out to lunch. I also notice that when I change suits for him he generally has his favorite brand in his pocket. It really is amusing to pull a pack of cigarettes from his pocket, having known him so long, that he did not smoke. Possibly, he will later take the same brand cigarettes and cigars his brother takes.

I was just upstairs to [see] Lieutenant Colonel Byllesby for the colonel and saw Lieutenant George Sunday, a son of the celebrated Rev. Billy Sunday that set the States on fire some time ago. He is one of the preachers who tells you something a little different from the other preachers.

The streets are all very dark at night and the store windows have large shutters that are pulled down to protect the glass in case of air raids, so you cannot do much window shopping in London at night.

They have as many large stores here as [in] New York or Philadelphia, and just as nice. They are up to the States in that line. The prices, I think are somewhat higher than in the States. At first, I had some trouble in getting on to this money and more than once it was necessary for the floor man to come and help the clerk out, because they don't know the value of the US money and I did not know the value of their money. The floor men have a book that gives both, and that way I would get fixed up. I think I lost some at first. But Mr. Houser and Smith have taught me about English money and I am now doing all right.

The Admiralty Arch stands at the Northeast corner of Hyde Park, which is called the Mall. Going straight past it you come to Buckingham Palace. It is one mile to it and a beautiful walk. All along are young trees, and a separate road for riding horses and autos to drive.

You will also pass a monument about a quarter of the way down dedicated to the soldiers that fell in the African War. It is quite large, and shaped like a half moon. Engraved on it are the names of the fallen. It has been very hard to get postcards of the things I have seen. Before America entered the war, England would not allow any [post]cards to go out of this country. Since we are in the war and helping them, it is now all right but the cards are hard to find, as they have run out and did not print others, so they say.

A little farther down the way you will pass the Marlborough House, which is very nice. It is a little hard to see, with so many trees and vines around it, unless you walk down by Pall Mall Street.

Next, you come to St. James Palace, right beside the St. James Park. Where on earth these people get all this money to build such places I wonder. At the time that these homes were built it must have been easier. I never saw such large and magnificent places in all my life.

During the autumn of 1913, using Portland Stone, Buckingham Palace was renovated based on designs by Royal Architect Sir Aston Webb. The portico and wings were given greater prominence by bringing them forward and tall pillars inserted between the windows from end to end, lending a dignity to the building which the former front lacked entirely. The palace derives its name for a mansion erected by John Sheffield, Duke of Buckingham in 1703, which was purchased by George II, some sixty years afterwards, when his family had out-grown St. James. His son and successor, George IV, commissioned his favorite architect, Nash, to remodel it.

But the palace was little used until 1837, when Queen Victoria chose it as her residence. King Edward VII made constant use of it as he had been born in the palace on the 9th of November 1841, and died here 6th May 1910. With the wing added [in] 1847 the palace forms an extensive quadrangle. The east front facing the park being 360 feet long. The king's private apartments are on the north side. No part of the palace is shown to the public.

When King George V and Queen Mary are in the residence the changing of the guards takes place here instead of St. James Place.

The changing of the guard takes place every morning at about 10:30 a.m. The band passes right by the office at the Belgrave Mansion with about one hundred and fifty soldiers. I look for them regularly and anticipate hearing them play. They look very good. They also have a drum corps with them. If the band is not playing the drum corps will be. But it is rare not to hear the band when passing here.

The gardens and lake at the back of the palace occupy about forty acres, between Constitution Hill and Grosvenor Place. The Royal Mews (this name is applied to the stables. The birds are kept in the

Mews or coops) are to the south of the Palace on Buckingham Palace Road. Here, too, is kept the magnificent state coach with paintings by Cipriani.

The speed limit around Buckingham Palace is twelve miles per hour. The roads and driveways are all very wide and the flowers are beautiful.

There is a soldier on guard at every gate. Each carries a gun with a bayonet on it. There is a small shelter for them to use in bad weather. There is also a soldier at every door in the yard. The palace is surrounded by an iron fence about ten feet high in the front, and the top is painted gold. I guess gilt, but it has the gold appearance anyhow.

I often go by the Royal Mews (stables) and look in the yard. I want to get a peep of the inside hut that is not allowed and particularly now during these war times.

At the gate, where the teams of horses come out, a butler stands wearing a bright red long Prince Albert coat, patent leather boots with white tops, and a high hat with white gloves. This is his dress all the time. When one butler goes off duty, another goes on wearing the same sort of an outfit.

The police officers are generally patrolling up and down Buckingham Palace Road very regularly.

The Buckingham Hotel, directly across the street, has been turned into a hospital for wounded soldiers. It is a very large hotel and finely situated.

All alleys here in London are paved and are kept very clean. In fact, the entire city is kept in very good order. The white wings here do very good work.

There are no trolley cars in the center of the city. The travelling is all done in the Trams. It is a bus of the double-decked kind like they have in New York. The fare runs from a pence to six and seven pence. They make very fair time, but you always feel as if you are going to topple over. I hear they do go over some times. They don't look safe to me. They have mostly women conductors now, as manpower is a little scarce. But if you look on the streets there seems to me many men still.

Trafalgar Square, so named in commemoration of Nelson's great victory, is a large open space, one of the finest sights in London, though it can hardly be said the best use has been made of it. On the southern or open side is the Nelson Monument, a granite column 145 feet high, surmounted by a statue of Admiral Horatio Nelson, 16 feet high.

On the base are bronze reliefs cast with the metal of captured French cannons.

Every year on the anniversary of the Trafalgar, October 21st, the monument is decked with wreaths and festoons in commemoration of the victory. During the war Trafalgar Square has been the scene of many recruitings, and a rallying place for all classes. There are also statues of Sir Henry Havelock, by William Behnes; Sir Charles J. Napier, by George Gamon Adams; General Charles Gordon, by Hamo Thronycroft; and George IV, by Sir Francis Legatt Chantrey. Below the parapet on the north side of the square and quite unknown to the majority of the Londoners are set out the Standard British Measures: Inch, Foot, Yard, Chain, etc. I was looking for this place last Sunday. I had seen the Square often but not the measures. I asked a man about fifty years old. He said he never heard of such a thing, that there was nothing to it. Well, I kept on walking and looking for it and I walked right up on it. There are brass plugs put right into concrete and the lengths are properly marked.

At the north side stands the St. Martin-in-Fields, sometimes known as the Admiralty Church.

Pews are reserved for the king and the Prince of Wales. All the children born of the Royal families are entered in the register. The church was erected between 1721–1726 by James Gibbs on the site of a former structure. The registry contains an entry of the baptism of Francis Bacon, 1561. Nell Gwynne is buried here.

As an office force, we have Field Clerk Mr. A. G. Houser, who served as secretary to Colonel M. C. Kennedy for fourteen years. He is now chief clerk, having had that experience in transportation matters. He is a valuable assistant to the colonel now.

He has only recently returned from Tours, France, where he was examined for second lieutenant, and it is likely he will soon be wearing the gold bar, which he very justly deserves. He is a good, honest and hard worker.

Mr. Houser was born and raised in Chambersburg. After graduating from Chambersburg Academy he went to work in the CV Railroad office and has been there since.

We also have as Assistant Secretary Mechanical Engineer Warren E. Smith of Brooklyn, New York. Mr. Smith is also trained in mechanical transportation matters having been for years a stenographer for President Flagler of the Florida East Coast Railway Company. He has only one regret and that is that his boss died so suddenly that he did not have time to mourn. Mrs. Flagler became so busy after husband No. 2 died that she did not mourn his loss. Mr. Smith has a real job on his hands. A young lady in New York State has got him just up to the pitch where he is willing to say "I will for life take you," and so on. Well, they are awful words and it is a long, heavy job. There are some very nice looking ladies in this building and they are looking very closely at Houser and Smith. Mr. Smith might be able to hold out, but it is a matter for him to decide. The pleasure is all his. He says he will marry the young lady just as soon as the war is over. I tell him to go to it, brother.

In the office adjoining ours, we have First Lieutenant Clarence T. Mackenson, who is chief clerk to Captain W. S. Franklin. In peace times, he is division freight agent of the Pennsylvania Rail Road, at Altoona. He received his early training with the Cumberland Valley as chief clerk to Mr. J. L. Eysmans, who was general freight agent of the CV, and was known as the live wire of the CV. Lieutenant Mackenson is always on the job and keeps the ball moving all the time. He is a hard worker and you can always find him at the right place at the right time. In fact, we all know when you have any training with the president of the CV, you either come up to the point or you [don't have a future with the CV].

Bicycles are very much used here both by men and women.

The news came across a few days ago that Miss Margaret R. Kennedy had a Red Cross benefit at "Ragged Edge" and cleared $250. They had dancing, swimming contests, pool, etc. The colonel said he often had dances when he was home but he always had to pay the bill. He did not know that they were going to turn "Ragged Edge" into a carrousel.

Sunday, August 18th, I thought I would go to the Westminster Abbey. I saw in the paper that the services began at 6:30 p.m. and that the doors opened at 6:00 p.m. So I was there on time and when the doors opened I was among the first to go in. I had been talking to a policeman, who told me to go way up front on the right-hand side so that I would be near the preacher. I went up to the seventh pew on the right-hand side; that was far enough for me. It was not the preacher so much that I wanted to hear or see. It was the church. All preachers tell you about the same story and in about the same way.

Promptly at 6:25 p.m. the chimes hit up a little tune for a few minutes then at 6:30 p.m. the organ broke loose and that music. Oh, it was simply great. They chanted the Apostles' Creed and it seemed that you could hear every voice in the choir separately. They sang so smoothly. Then the minister showed up and read from the Bible. I did not hear what chapter it was, I was looking at the statues, but he did not read very long. Then he walked away from a small pulpit or rostrum. Then the choir chanted some more and at exactly 6:50 p.m., he started to preach and he stopped at exactly 7:15 p.m. That was plenty long enough, as you know men do not care for long sermons. Short ones do just as much good. I think his sermon was from some place in St. Luke. I know it was Saint somebody, anyhow.

Then the choir sang and shortly someone touched me on the shoulder. I looked around and a lady was handing me a sort of a pocket book. It was about six inches square lined with red plush and had beadwork on the outside. It had a little handle on about two inches long. I then understood that money was wanted. I put my hand in my pocket and thought I had what I wanted, and it proved to be a shilling. Not wishing to hold the precious thing I dropped the coin and passed it to the gentleman beside me. I looked to see how much he was going to put in and he put in three pence. Well there, I said to myself, "Stung again." But they say God loves the cheerful give, and that seems to be all I have been doing since I hit London.

They pass this collection book around and finally they get it up to the altar, and the ushers meet there and they do some chanting and then sing "Abide With Me." Oh, that was simply beautiful.

After the church was dismissed, the people next to me began to talk to me. They asked me if I had ever been in the church before. I said, "No, Miss." They told me to look around. I thought it was not allowed on Sunday. They were both elderly people and the gentleman spoke up and said he lived in London all his life and this was the first time in Westminster Abbey for him. The other lady I had found was his sister and she said, "Yes, I am always after him to come along to church, but he always has some excuse." Well, I was not after any family history, so I began asking questions about the church, and I did ask some.

The lady could tell you almost anything about the structure and the sights were the most wonderful I ever saw, or I guess ever will see. It really is hardly worthwhile for me to try to describe this wonderful church, for I do not have the "what" is needed to express it.

I counted forty-one statues in the main part and thought that was all. It wasn't half. When they took me around the left wing, I saw statues of dukes, lords, earls, and all went well until I happened to look on the floor, which is made of concrete. I saw some kind of brass letters and from the shape they looked like a coffin. I asked the lady what they were. "Oh, yes," she said. "They are the graves of dukes, kings, earls, and lords." Well, you should have seen me step aside. She said that is all right to walk there but every time I took a step I was looking to see what and where I was walking. It might have been all right for her but I am not caring to be much around the dead.

I did not know until later that you could buy any literature of the church. I wrote in my hat the number of statues. I have since bought a book telling the history of the church.

I overlooked saying the church dismissed at 7:40 p.m. and when you get out of the church it is near 8:30 p.m. I was much surprised at the congregation. It was very ordinary and not the aristocracy I had thought it would be. Many soldiers were there. I was the only gentleman of color that was there.

Tuesday evening, August the 13th, Colonel M. C. Kennedy gave a dinner at 14 Great Cumberland Place in honor of Lieutenant Colonel D. B. Wentz[1] of Tours, France. Colonel Wentz is a director of the Franklin National Bank of Philadelphia, and the knowledge that he is from there alone puts a feeling on a waiter.

Those present: Colonel M. C. Kennedy, Lieutenant Colonel D. B. Wentz, Lieutenant Colonel H. M. Byllesby,[2] Colonel S. G. Jones, Major J. E. Dunning, Sir Guy Colthrop, Naval Constructor Mr. L. B. McBride, Captain W. S. Franklin, Mr. E. Land of the Navy.

The dinner was a great success and all present were wonderfully pleased. Mr. McBride touched the lights at the proper time and all were seated and what was said made all feel happy.

These affairs go a long way in the war effort to bottling up the kaiser. After the war, it will be seen that the dinners at 14 Great Cumberland Place had a lot to do with the downfall of Germany.

1. Prior to the war, Daniel Bertsch (D. B.) Wentz (1872–1926) served as president of the Stonega Coke and Coal Company headquartered out of Philadelphia, Pennsylvania.
2. Lieutenant Colonel Henry Marison Byllesby (1859–1924) was the founding partner of the Pittsburgh-based H. M. Byllesby & Associates, an amalgamation of gas and electric companies.

Ice water was passed at the proper time, and once more the colonel smoked his favorite brand of cigarettes.

When the guests arrived, Lieutenant Colonel Byllesby came in an auto with Major Dunning. After opening the door, Major Dunning saw me he said, "By God, Colonel Byllesby, he is here." Then said to me, "Roy, we have heard lots of you." Surely, when people way up in the world like these men speak of a servant, who could but try to make good.

Later on in the dinner he said, "I see, Roy, you understand how to take care of we fellows. You have handled the dinner very nicely," Colonel Wentz said the same. But wait until they appear at "Ragged Edge," then they will see service. These houses were built when they first said, "Let us build a house." And I don't think a nail has been put in since they were put up. All right for that time but things have now changed. Oh, well, I will see them up the Cumberland Valley later on.

It was thought that Captain Franklin would step over and smoke once but he would not yield.

Captain Franklin is a quiet thinker, but he sees and always hears everything that is going on.

Hampton Court Place. No visitor to London, no matter how pressed for time, should fail to see the beautiful and stately palace built for Cardinal Wolsey for his own delight and afterwards "presented"—not very willingly we must believe—to his Royal Master Henry VIII. It is the largest and in many respects the finest of all the royal palaces in England, though it has not been occupied by a sovereign since the time of George II. It contains about 1,000 apartments, of which four-fifths are occupied by royal pensioners and privileged persons.

The Courts and the charming gardens are open to all. In 1910, the old moat was opened up and a fine battlement bridge built by Henry VIII for his "own darling" Anne Boleyn was disclosed, after being buried for centuries.

One of the sights in the gardens is the great vine planted [in] 1768, which I am told after a period of great poverty is again yielding abundantly. In 1909, it won the silver medal from the Royal Horticultural Society. I had often seen these large red grapes and wondered what kind of a vine they grew on. Well, I have now seen these vines. This vine has a great many bunches hanging on. They are the very large blue grapes that are sold by the pound and are very expensive.

The vine is several feet in diameter and covers a very large space. The home park of six hundred acres is bound on all sides by the Thames River. Many of the trees are said to be over two hundred years old.

There are many buildings, streets, theatres, apartment houses, hotels, business houses, named after Queen Victoria, or some of the king's children. In fact, I think if the king just looked at a store the owner would put up a sign reading "Purveyor to His Majesty."

The saloons and restaurants close at 9:00 p.m. and these people, the women as well as the men, are some drinkers. Nearly any time you pass a saloon you can see the women standing right at the bar drinking with the men. They mostly drink ale and I have not seen a half dozen drunken people since I have been here.

The saloons also open up on Sunday evenings for about two hours, from five to seven. They all have bar maids, as men are scarce now.

It is nothing to see the soldiers kissing the maids over the bar. I saw two kissing the same girl at Piccadilly the other night. She was a real fair looking blonde. They are not slow taking a kiss. Maybe the American soldiers have not gotten to this place but the girls are rather crazy over cigarettes. Why they are wild? Crazy for an American cigarette. You can see them in taxis, and in the opera house between acts. Recently, I saw two walking on the street, in Oxford Circus, smoking them. In the office building, I see some of them puff while they are hammering the typewriter. Oh it is the real thing now, this cigarette habit.

You never see a service flag over here on any house and really very few of any other kinds of flags. These people just seem to take this war in a matter of fact way. When it is over, they will win.

And on they go fighting right along.

August 5th was bank holiday and everybody laid off. The miners would not work, so boats were held up for coal. They had to have their holiday. And as for strikes, this place has got them all skint. If you look at these people hard they strike. About the middle of August, the women conductors went on strike over wages. They wanted the same as the men received. They were out several days, and that is the shortest way to travel to the stores. Well, they settled that in about a week. Then the conductors on the Underground Railways went out for three days and then the police got up a row and they were out two days. Mr. Lloyd George got them straightened out and they went back on the job. Now the Gas employees are talking about going out. One thing, these people don't fight or get fussy. They just simply stop until they get what they want.

I came down from the Hampden Court by the boat Connaught, down the Thames. It is one of the most beautiful rides one can take. I counted twenty-eight boathouses along the river. They were simply fine. I have never seen anything so near them except those at the Lake Geneva. I often wonder how the little children don't fall into the water. They play right in the deck with only a small rope around as a fence. How the people keep their cellar dry with the yard right up against the Thames I would like to know. Coming down the Thames you go through two locks. One at Paddington where your boat goes in the lock and you take a fall of fifteen feet. Then the gate is opened and you sail out in the river again and you come to the Richmond lock, where you take a fall of about four feet. It takes about twenty minutes to make that drop in the locks. It is very simple after you once see it. And is on the same order of the Panama Canal only on a smaller scale. The lawns along the river look just like a picture.

After coming through the second lock you head straight for Westminster where you dock. It takes four hours and thirty minutes to make the trip and the fare is two shillings (50 cents). We left Hampton Court at 4:30 p.m. and arrived at Westminster at 8:15 p.m.

While I admit the women are a cranky set in most cases, I must admit that they will work. They have here a society called the WAACs. Well, some funny things are being said about them. They are willing to take a man's place in many things. It is said they go up behind the firing line, to comfort and help. There are about six hundred of them and they wear dove colored dresses and have the word WAAC sewed on the arm in blue letters. They make a very presentable body when they turn out and, well, they are doing their bit.

Most of the porters at the train stations are now women. They handle the baggage, use the trucks, call taxicabs, and handle the manly work. I see nearly every day three women digging in the street with a pick and shovel. The women here are not afraid to work.

Most of the delivery wagons and trucks are driven by women. And the milk wagons here consist of a cart with a can that will hold about fifteen gallons. They push and pull over a certain territory in the mornings delivering milk. They always carry the milk into the house. Never deposit it on the steps.

On Monday, Colonel M. C. Kennedy dined at the American Luncheon Club with the Honorable Franklin D. Roosevelt, the assistant secretary of the Navy, USA.[3] The assistant secretary made a brief speech that made a good impression.

The same evening he attended a private dance given at the home of General John Biddle and among those he met there were the Duchess of Marlborough, Mrs. Willing Astor, Lord and Lady Leigh, and His Highness, the Duke of Connaught.

At 12:45 a.m. today, Brigadier General Henry W. Thornton called to have Colonel Kennedy take lunch with him. He said to me, "Boy, I have heard lots about you and I am glad you got over safely." General Thornton is an American but has been in England now for some years teaching these people here how to run railroads.

He was general manager of the Long Island Railroad. He is now brigadier general of the British Army and is also general manager of the Eastern Railway since 1914, engineer-in-chief, deputy director of Inland Waterways and Docks, assistant director general of Movements and Railways. He was born at Logansport, Ind., USA, November 6, 1871. He attended St. Paul's School, Concord, New Hampshire, USA, University of Pennsylvania, entered service of the PRR 1894, Engineering Department. Various positions in the office of chief engineer, division engineer, division superintendent, general superintendent until he came abroad. Clubs: London Wall, Junior Athenaeum, Royal Automobile, Queens, Mid-Surrey Golf, and Lotus.

I went over to Victoria Station this afternoon, to get the evening papers. It really looks very sad to see the mothers with small children in their arms, seeing their husbands and fathers off. They are going back to the front, no telling if he will return or not. The people seem to stand up real well. They hug and kiss their parents goodbye. Like Sherman said of war, "it's hell."

Colonel Shartle of the good old Cumberland Valley dropped in to say, "How are you" to our colonel today. He just came over from the States. He looks very well.

---

3. Franklin Delano Roosevelt (1882–1945) served as the assistant secretary of the navy from 1913 until 1920. He would go on to become the thirty-second president of the United States (1933–1945), winning a record four elections before dying in office.

On Saturday afternoon, August 31st, Colonel Kennedy told me to get him a taxi and have it at the front of headquarters at 1:45 p.m. Generally you have a little trouble in getting taxis, as there do not seem to be enough to go around.

Well, I had gotten one and was talking to him to hold him for the colonel, when I happened to look up the street and I saw a walk that looked very familiar to me. I looked closely and saw it was Lieutenant T. B. Wood of Chambersburg. Well, I waited until he came up to the door. I touched him on the sleeve and said, "How are you, Mr. "Wood?" He turned around and said, "Why my God, Roy, what are you doing over here?" I said, "I am here with Colonel Kennedy." He said, "Where is he?" I pointed him out. They recognized each other at about the same time and the handshake they took was great.

I was glad to be on hand at the proper time and place. Colonel Kennedy was going away in a taxi with Colonel Proctor. Major Lieutenant Wood made arrangements to see the colonel in the morning. After the colonel and party had gone he turned and said to me "Roy, when did you land here?" I said, "August third." He said, "When did you see my mother?" I said, "July fifteenth. She was sitting on the porch as I passed on my way to the train." He said, "Was she well?" I said, "Yes sir, she looked very well." He said, "I am glad to hear that." And you can be sure I was glad to be able to give that much information to someone from home.

Lieutenant Wood looked very well and it certainly made a fellow think he was home to meet someone from the "old Burg" that they knew so well.

He has been sent to London to buy various tools for the American Army. I will surely be glad to see and hear more of him in the morning.

In the evening Lieutenant Colonel Byllesby gave a dinner in the dining room of the Ritz Hotel to Samuel Gompers.[4] The other guests were J. H. Frey, of the Molders Union; Edgar Wallace, representing the miners; William J. Bowen, president of the Bricklayers Union; C. L. Baine, secretary, Boot and Shoe Workers Union; Guy H. Oyster, US Labor Mission; General Biddle; Colonel M. C. Kennedy; Colonel Powell.

This Labor Commission is here presumably to encourage the British workman to renew their efforts. The labor situation here in England is far from satisfactory. Strikes are common and labor is very independent

4. Samuel Gompers (1850–1924) was an American labor leader and founder of the American Federation of Labor (AFL).

and arbitrary. There is constant trouble with the miners and the situation is most serious. Skilled labor for the erection of hospitals is also very scarce and difficult to secure.

The idea was, I think, to make a large boost in all production lines and that the concentrated effort would hasten the ending of the war.

Saturday night I went to see Madame Tussaud's exhibition of wax works. It was the best show of its kind I have ever seen. I saw all but Napoleon's Room, which I will see later.

I was certainly surprised to see Liszt, Gounod, Verdi, Wagner, and many others of the world's greatest musical artists. They looked as if they could speak.

Lieutenant Wood called and had a long conversation with the colonel this morning and will dine at the mess this evening.

I was at St. Paul's Cathedral Sunday evening. It is some church. Much larger than the Abbey, but a much younger church. It, too, has concrete

Royal A. Christian visited St. Paul's Cathedral frequently while in London. On November 12, 1918, King George V and Queen Mary attended a thanksgiving service to celebrate the end of the war, in which more than 700,000 British soldiers died. A majority of those leaving St. Paul's are women. Courtesy of the National Archives and Record Administration, College Park, Maryland, 3819[266D8]

floors. The choir is composed of boys nearly all under fifteen years of age. The music is wonderful. There seemed to be something in the rear of the church that I did not see. Many people were coming from the rear saying it was nice. I will be in this church many times. Next time, I will get in earlier.

They have several men in this church that have V. A. D. marked on their breast and they carry a sort of a soldier's canteen on their side filled with water. Two women and one man fainted in the church. They carried them out, and some people in the church said they only wanted to be carried in some man's arms, that you could not see them kicking any, that they were satisfied as soon as a man took hold of them.

Sunday morning, September 15th, Lieutenant T. B. Wood dropped in to see Colonel Kennedy and spent from 10:30 a.m. until noon with him and later took dinner with the colonel at 14 Great Cumberland Place. I met Lieutenant Wood Monday morning and he took me with him to his office, which is above the American garage in Pembroke Mews, just off Chapel Street, on the fourth floor. He has a very nice, cozy little office there and he had bought a tool for the colonel, which I brought back for him.

Lieutenant Wood is stationed at Nevers, France, but as orders are still coming in to him to get more tools for the army, he says he cannot tell how much longer he will be in London.

He has not received mail from home for some time, due principally to the fact that he is moved around so much that it does not get to follow him.

I was at the house at 14 Great Cumberland Place on Sunday evening and made up for the gentlemen a few of those things that always make you feel sorta dignified. You know. And they enjoyed their dinner all the more.

On Monday morning, US secretary of war Newton Baker and General Hines dropped in to see Colonel Kennedy and were here in the office from 10:00 a.m. until 11:55 a.m.

On Monday afternoon, September 16th, Mr. James Wideman (J. W.) Lee, a brother of Mr. Ivy Lee and who has visited in the Cumberland Valley, called to see the colonel and also took dinner at 14 Great Cumberland Place that evening.

Tuesday, Secretary of War Newton Baker and General Hines called again to see Colonel Kennedy, who had Captain Franklin attend. They met for some time. I understand they snapped a photograph of him in

US secretary of war Newton D. Baker leaves the YMCA Morn Hill in Winchester, England, in September 1918. He traveled to Europe to visit the American Expeditionary Forces, inspecting the transportation and supply lines and touring encampments to boost the morale of American troops. Courtesy of the National Archives and Records Administration, College Park, Maryland, 25348[1102T8]

front of the American Army Headquarters, but I have not been able to see it in any of the pictorial papers.

There are very, very few homes here that have furnaces in them. They nearly all have fireplaces. In this hotel, which is one of the largest, they have fireplaces in every room, and right across the street I see fifteen chimneys in one home. They burn soft coal and it will keep a room very comfortable.

There is a very great deal of thought being given about the coal consideration for this winter. Many persons think there will be a shortage.

Between Downing Street and the Treasury Building is the Horse Guards and two mounted sentries changed every hour. These guards sit on black horses and in formal dress. There is always somebody standing looking at them. They really do look fine. Right behind this is the Horse Guards Parade Ground, where they take part in the changing of the Guard every morning at 10:30 a.m.

They also have a play they play on the "Official" birthday of the king they call "Trooping the Color" that takes place in the rear of the Horse Guards Whitehall. They change guards every morning at 10:30 a.m.

Now right in front of the Hotel Cecil along the Victoria Embankment is the "Cleopatra's Needle." On the last night of the German air raid they were after the Cecil Hotel, as the Royal Air Force (RAF) headquarters are on the top floor of the hotel, and in dropping bombs they hit the steps of the monument, the walk was broken up in many places and several holes were knocked in the statues that are on the side of this monument. I was down there and was shown the different places that had been hit.

This Victoria Embankment starts at the Westminster Bridge and runs for a mile and a half. There is a double-decked trolley that runs the whole way and it is a beautiful ride. It extends clear to Blackfriars Bridge. It is one of the finest and most air-swept thoroughfares in the Metropolis, with attractive gardens, beautiful buildings, and an always interesting view of the River Thames. The granite protecting wall is eight feet thick.

Throughout its length the embankment is planted on both sides with shade trees, and it is lit at night by electricity but during the war times they have very low candlepower lights on and it is very dark along that line.

Beneath the embankment runs the district railway with stations Westminster Bridge, Charing Cross, the Temple, and beneath the Thames, it connects with the Hampton Tube. On the embankment facing the station is a bronze medal by Sir G. Frampton, R. A. of Sir W. S. Gilbert, the playwright, whose "foe was folly and his weapon wit."

Turning in the direction of the Westminster Bridge, we pass through pretty gardens decked with statues of General Sir Francis Outram, the "Bayard" of the Indian Mutiny, Sir Bartle Frere of South African fame and William Tyndale, the translator of the New Testament. Next comes Montague House, the Mansion of Duke Buccleuch. A few yards beyond is the dignified building of Scottish Baronial style, known as the New Scotland Yard, the headquarters since 1891 of the Metropolitan Police, the lost property office, etc.

The House of Parliament is also right adjoining Westminster Bridge. I had hesitated to speak of it, as I thought I was going to have a look inside. But when I strolled by recently and talked to some man at the door, I was told no one was admitted during war times. So, I guess

I should just as well say what I have seen from the outside, as there does not seem to be any way for me to see the inside.

The clock in the tower is called "Big Ben." It has four dials [faces], each twenty-two and one-half feet in diameter. It was constructed by Edward J. Dent under the direction of the late Lord Grimthorpe. It is one of the finest time-keepers in the world. The minute hands are fourteen feet long, the hour hands nine feet long, and the figures are two feet long. The minute spaces are one foot square. The clock is called "Big Ben" as a compliment to Sir Benjamin Hall, who was first commissioner of works at the time the Bell was cast. It weighs thirteen and one-half tons and in calm weather its clear note may be heard over the greater part of London. The quarters are struck on four smaller bells. The central tower is three hundred feet high, and is used as a ventilating shaft. The Great Victoria Tower on the southeast is three hundred thirty-six feet high and seventy-five feet square. The archway beneath is fifty feet high and forms the royal entrance, which is used by the king and queen in opening Parliament. Beyond the archway are the Victoria flower gardens.

The House of Lords is directly across from the House of Parliament. I will not write about what I have seen of that yet as there may be some way for me to get inside. If I find there is not, I will write up the outside as I see it.

On Thursday afternoon, Lieutenant Colonel D. B. Wentz and Lieutenant Commander John S. Higgins planned to go to Cardiff, Wales. However, after Colonel Wentz was assigned new orders, he could not go. I was sent in a hurry up trip to head off Commander Higgins. I found him taking things easy at the Paddington Station, walking up and down smoking pure Havana cigars. They are very scarce here. Dinner had been ordered for him and Colonel Wentz, but all was cancelled and I came back to 14 Great Cumberland Place in a taxi with Commander Higgins. He has had some wonderful trips and some more are planned. There was one time he had wished for me while he and the other officers were getting me across. What did he have in mind for me? Nothing would please me more. I can hardly wait until another opportunity comes again.

He will take the matter up with Colonel Kennedy and Captain Franklin, and here is hoping I can be spared for that, as it is just what I had planned in my mind from last January until the present time. I will surely thank them and will surely make good.

The stations here in London are always crowded. Commander Higgins tells me the Germans have tried very hard to bomb Paddington Station, but as yet not successful in reaching it, but I hear they have been near it on several of their raids. We are giving them a merry chase now and they must cover pretty soon.

Well, I just came from the Westminster Cathedral. This is Sunday night, September 22nd, and right while it is fresh in my mind I will write it up. It is considered one of the largest churches in London and I can say it is not far wrong. I went in at 6:45 p.m. and after looking around for about ten minutes I took a seat about the fourteenth row. At three minutes of seven some kind of bells rang—they had a very sort of light ring to them. Then at seven promptly the organ began. It played for only a short time, and then they began to chant something. A lot of people were coming in. I noticed how they kneeled down for a few minutes then took a seat. But one or two knelt for an awful long time. I do not know what that was for. It could be that you go according to the amount of sins committed the week. But, I won't touch that part.

Then they chanted again. There are two men wearing red coats that sit way up in the choir. I noticed whenever they stood up the parishioners did the same; but at other times they did not. To me, there seemed to be a great deal of rising and sitting throughout the service.

The singing was not to me so good. You cannot understand the singing like in other churches. I guess it was of some high order. Probably too rich for me. But I thought there was so much chanting. The minister or priest, I guess he is called, began to preach or speak at 7:25 p.m. and he talked pretty good about preparing in time, etc. He wore a little dark cap and a sort of cape of light color around his shoulders, and he did not use a Bible. He seemed to have what he was going to talk on committed to memory, and he had a pretty good delivery. I got some of it. It was mostly along the usual line. Then the choir began to stir about and light candles. He concluded at 7:40 p.m. Good timing I thought. Several men in white gowns walked out in front of the candles. The choir is composed of boys wearing a sort of a dark skirt and real long white capes.

There are also voices that sound like there are ladies in the choir but there are none to be seen. They are all men and boys. Finally, two men began to lift the collection. I saw them coming so I got my contribution out early that I might make no mistake. This time I put in four pennies of the English kind. I also noticed that he had more of them than he had in silver. The large brass plate he is carrying is about the size of a dinner plate, with carvings of something all around. He used two hands to carry it. I guess it was heavy with all the large pennies. The American soldiers call it "iron money." At any rate they went over the church carefully and seemed to get all that was loose. Then they disappeared, money and all. I saw nothing more of them during the remainder of the service.

Books are sold at the church right after service on Sunday. I bought a book and cards. They have an office there where these are sold at the entrance of the church.

In the basement of the church, they have a crypt, which I think is a sort of a vault. I am not sure, but I will not see that if it is.

In the right-hand side is the pulpit where the priest speaks from and at all the archways come into a large aisle that would seat many hundred people. I must admit, these people do know how to build churches. The interior is of brick. No plaster work at all, and there are many columns of fine marble all along the aisles.

The choir sits in front of the cross in the rear. There are six beautiful candles about five feet high, which burn all the time. They light two clusters of twelve candles on each side and sit on the steps directly under the cross.

It makes a fine sight. Everybody seems to be on and understand their job. On each side of the main hall are rooms called the Lady Chapel. These are used for Sunday school rooms. Each has chairs that are light and very comfortable. These side rooms are plastered, but the main part of the church is not.

I do not know how they keep these places warm in real winter weather. If the winter here is anything like it was in the Cumberland Valley last year, it will be some more jobs.

On all the arches are drawings of saints, virgins, apostles, and confessors. They are in white and a gold cross at the head, in a sort of a square about four feet.

There are a great many dinners given by the officers attached to this station. And among them was one that was very much talked of: the dinner given by Sir Sam Fay, director general of Movements and Railways, at Hotel Savoy, August 20th, 1918.

Those present were: Mr. S. M. Felton, director general of American Military Railways; Major General Sir W. T. Furse, KCB, DSO, master general of the Ordinance; Lieutenant General Hutchinson, CB, DSO, director of organization War Office; Brigadier General H. O. Mance, CB, CMG, DSO, director of Railways and Roads; Brigadier General O. H. Delano Osborn, CMG, director of Movements; Major General P. P. deB. Radcliffe, CB, DSO, director of Military Operations; Sir Francis Dent, general manager of the South Eastern and Chatham Rwy.; Colonel M. C. Kennedy, RTC, USA, deputy director general of Transportation in England; Captain H. M. Paul, ADC to director general of Movements and Railways.

An extract from the *New York Times* of August 3, 1918, says:

A very wide circle of friends in America will welcome a word of news from Colonel M. C. Kennedy, President of the Cumberland Valley Railway, one of the Pennsylvania Lines, by the way, the only railroad that has no bonds outstanding. At his lovely home in the Cumberland Valley, Colonel Kennedy has for years held an annual party to which hundreds of railroad heads and bankers were invited. His hospitality is famous. He is now Deputy Director General of Transportation of the American Expeditionary Forces under General Atterbury.

Colonel Kennedy (the silver eagles on his shoulders to authorize the title) is in full charge in England. He is ably assisted by Capt. W. S. Franklin, of Baltimore, a younger brother of the head of the International Mercantile Marine Company. Colonel Kennedy is delighted at the opportunity of serving his country abroad and it is particularly agreeable to be associated with his old colleague Atterbury, who was vice-president and general manager of the Pennsylvania.

In April, among the first troops that came over the king handed to each soldier a letter which they appreciated very much and it was the talk of the American soldiers for several days as to how to get them home and at the same time have them as a souvenir from His Majesty, the King.

On Friday, September 20th, Colonel M. C. Kennedy gave a dinner at his home, 14 Great Cumberland Place in honor of Captain Cone, of the Navy, and Colonel D. B. Wentz, of the AEF, Tours, France.

Those present were: Colonel M. C. Kennedy, Lieutenant Colonel D. B. Wentz, Captain H. I. Cone, Major J, E. Dunning, Major White, Mr. L. B. McBride.

The dinner was a decided success and there was used for the first time a beautiful article that was presented to Colonel Kennedy by Colonel Wentz. The "shaker" was used that night and all went off all right but it was seen that the holes were not quite large enough for the "Bronx" as made in the States. It was then decided that Roy should take it to Goldsmith and Silversmith where it was purchased and have the holes made a little larger.

In the *London Times*, which is the leading daily paper here, they have a place says "Events of the Day." I have been watching it for some time. I read that on Thursday the king was going to hold "Investiture" at Buckingham Palace. That means that the king will decorate persons with VC, MM, DSO and many other degrees, to those who have done some act of importance for their country. I was particularly anxious to see this done. I had planned all kinds of ways up until this time, so Thursday morning I bring the shaker with me to the office, and at 10:25 a.m. I start for the Jeweler, which is on Regent Street, near Piccadilly Circus, and down past Buckingham Road. I had heard that they would allow you to see this exercise so I went up to the Buckingham Palace Gate with the package securely wrapped in my arm. The guard asked me, "What have you in that package? Anything out of the ordinary?" I said, "No sir, it is a cocktail shaker. I am on my way to the jeweler to have it fixed." He said, "All right, you go ahead." Well, in went Roy with Colonel Wentz's cocktail shaker close to my heart, for I knew if I allowed anything to happen to it I should just as well go jump off the Westminster Bridge. The guard laughed at me when I told him what I had in my arm, but that did not stop me. I kept going. When I got through the second gate to the place where they have the exercises, I was satisfied. Well, it turned out to be one of the greatest days for Roy.

There is a platform erected about fifteen feet wide and thirty feet long covered with a red and white awning. There are three officers with the king. Each is dressed in khaki with red trimmings. I do not yet know the name of the dress of the king but will have it before I finish this story. One gentleman on the platform is wearing a long Prince Albert coat, black, with black shoes, his hat off, steel colored trousers.

The person that is to be decorated walks up the platform and steps in front of the king. He stops, stands at attention and salutes the king. The king returns the salute. The other officer reads to the people that are gathered the act that the person has done to be so honored and the crowd cheers and applauds. I did, too. Then the king puts on him the prize that he is entitled to. If it is a VC the king pins it on his breast, pats him on the head or shoulder, and says a few words of encouragement to him. The recipient stands at attention, he then salutes the king who returns the gesture. After dismissing him, the next recipient follows.

The king generally shakes the hand of everyone. Sometimes he, as he did this morning, puts a collar of scarlet on the heads of several gray-haired men. He patted them on the shoulder. I noticed there is a sort

Royal A. Christian's Consular registration card dated September 23, 1918. As a US citizen living in England, Christian had to provide information related to his occupation, his employer, and the location of his employment. Registration state: Pennsylvania; Registration county: Franklin; Roll: 1892183; Draft board: 2. Ancestry.com, US, World War I Draft Registration Cards (c. 1917–1918). Provo, Utah, Ancestry. com Operations Inc., 2005. Courtesy of the National Archives and Record Administration, College Park, Maryland of balcony all around the courtyard and on these the queen and some of her lady friends look on at the exercises. A policeman I was standing next to told me just where the queen was sitting. She had sort of a purple dress on and a very nice looking lady near her had a cream colored dress on. The officer did not know the name. I was sorry.

As I was on an errand, I could not see it all play out. I was there long enough to see how it was done. I then caught a bus and finished the errand I was on. But, ain't that something, from being a messenger boy at Cumberland Valley Railroad, Chambersburg to Buckingham Palace and see the king going through this exercise. In my mind I was "Going Some."

Many of the older men who have done something deserving of recognition from their country and are so honored have their wives with them. Of course, the wives do not go along on the platform with them but they are present, and it is amusing how dear they seem to hold their husbands after he has been so honored by the king. I guess that is about all the peace some of them have at home for a few days. This morning the king put a very great many collars on elderly men and officers of the RAF.

In the same afternoon the king inspects the Great Italian Band (Carabinieri) that is here this week. Wednesday was Italian Day in London. The band played several pieces at mass at the Westminster Cathedral. I did not get to hear them there, but when they broke loose at the Buckingham Palace at 1:30 p.m. this afternoon, I was right there. I waited until 1:25 p.m. to go to lunch and once outside the door to Buckingham Palace I went. When they started out, I became one of the crowd.

It is some band. It played in the Quadrangle, which is the end near the office building. They had two sets of drums and cymbals, and I cannot tell the different kinds of horns, but at any rate you know they played their best for the king. And as I was there, naturally they played their best to my hearing. So this is the day I call "Roy's day at Buckingham Palace."

On Wednesday, Colonel Kennedy and Captain Franklin went to Southampton to look at the docks and etc. They were gone all day. Today, there is a strike on hand. Soldiers that want to report for duty are compelled to find some other way to get back to duty and as I have said, this is the rankest country for strikes you ever saw. The main stations did not have one train moving.

I learned that the Italian Band plays in Hyde Park on Sunday afternoon and I will be sure to hear it again. If you could have seen the crowd on the streets yesterday as they passed several places, you would not have thought there was any war going on.

Yesterday afternoon, Saturday, September 28th, while passing the Royal Mews, I had a little talk with the guard, after which I was taken through the Royal Stables. How this was accomplished need not be put in print, as everything done on this side would not look good in print. I saw what I wanted and when you read this account, I think you will say I saw pretty near all.

When all the horses are in the stables there are one hundred and forty in all. Some are now at the Windsor Castle, the summer home of the king.

There are now about one hundred and ten horses in the Mews, and most of them are bay horses. They have large rugs along the side of the stall to prevent a horse from rubbing himself. The names of all horses are painted above their stalls. There is plenty of straw to keep them clean, and they are really very well groomed.

I got pictures of the yard that circles the Royal Mews, giving plenty of air and light. The "State Landau" is used by the king to attend small affairs in and about the city. This vehicle is also used by a member of the king's household, and only teamed with two black horses. In the summer, the king uses his Windsor Greys, a team that he always takes with him to his summer house at Windsor.

The persons who showed me through the stables said that the king and queen are very fond of horses, and that both ride very often. In the rear of the stalls is a sort of straw mat and the floor is made of concrete. The mat is about eight inches wide and is rough at the other end.

Each horse is tied with two chains and is kept with blanket on. The stables are the warmest I have ever been in. Each felt as though there were stoves in them. The stables are all lighted with electricity and gas.

I saw a harness of Red Morocco, said to cost 17,000 pounds, which was used for four pairs of cream-colored horses that draw the king's State Coach. They also have the same number of sets of black harness, which they use on a set of black horses, which they told me cost the same. They have a harness room about forty feet long and about twenty-five feet wide. All harnesses hang on frames. The brass on the harness is very heavy and is well polished. I was told was in case one of the cream horses was sick, the black ones could be used.

The State Coach is used for the opening of the Parliament by the king and queen and also for coronations, when they use it they have six footmen. If some others use it they have four coachmen, and to others they use two. But it is never used with less than two footmen.

The wheels in the rear of this coach are six feet one inch in diameter and are dished in. I cannot recall how old it was nor would be able to say how much it cost, but I think I am on the inside now and I will get that information in another way.

A coal black horse, with the exception of a white mark on the right hind foot, is the favorite riding horse of the king. It was presented to him by the Australian government, and has won the Epsom Downs Derby. His name is "Delhi" which is painted above his stall.

A light bay horse is Princess Mary's favorite riding horse, but I cannot now recall its name.

There is a large riding stable in the rear of this Mews where the Royal children and their friends are taught to ride. It is about one hundred and thirty feet long and about seventy feet wide. It was about twice that size before the war but they have cut about the half of it off and made beds in it for soldiers who on going to or returning from the front have no friends or places to stay. They now have seventy beds in the part next to this riding stable. It is very high. They also have all kinds of horns, drums, whistles, and make all manner of noises to help the horses become accustomed to these things, so they do not scare when they are on the streets.

As far as I could see, the other horses are ordinary looking horses. I was very glad to be able to see these stables, and am very grateful to the gentleman who showed me through them.

There is a small house, but quite high in the rear of Buckingham Palace. The person said that this was Queen Victoria's summer home and that any time, the queen wanted to know the character of any of her servants or anyone else around the place, she would go into this house and look out the windows. There were windows all around the house. They could not see her but she could see all that was going on. The lady that told me talked as if she knew all about it. There is no question that she could see a very great deal without being seen. I guess she was right foxy in some ways. Well, possibly she had to be. People with so many servants around have to see a great many things, she said. Of course, she said, there are other people that one must look after too. I judge she knew from where she spoke, and I left it at that and asked no questions along that line.

I think I have had a pretty good experience at Buckingham Palace this week.

When you see the flag on the pole over Buckingham Palace you know the king is at home, for whenever he goes away the flag is taken down.

The news continued to come in good from the front and everybody around here is wise to what the end will be.

Charing Cross Hotel and station are just past Trafalgar Square near what is called the beginning of the Strand, which is considered the busiest part of London. To me, London looks very busy all over. They surely do some business in this city, and I cannot see where all the people come from.

There are many relics of the Germans that have been taken by the French on exhibition on the Strand. It seems that no cards showing them can be bought.

While it is not just ripe yet, there is a terrible lot of dissatisfaction among the mail carriers over their rate of pay and it will not surprise anyone if they don't strike for several days. As I have said before, these are striking people.

Sunday, October 6th, 1918, I thought I would take a walk around to Trafalgar Square and see how things are coming around for the show they will have there during the week to sell war bonds.

From there, I went to see the Great Scotland Yards, which is just off from Parliament Street.

Scotland Yard is a large white building in the rear of Hotel Metropole. There is a street that runs from White Hall to Parliament Street that is called Great Scotland Yard. This is where the building gets its name. All records of criminals are kept there. As well as all lost articles that are found and are turned in are sent there. The owners can regain them after identifying them. It is said that one-half of the articles that are lost in London are returned in this way to their owners. That speaks well for London. I hardly believe that happens in any city of the US. The articles that are not called for or redeemed after having been kept for a period of three months are given to the persons that turned them in.

I then went to see Mr. Lloyd George's home at 10 Downing Street. Downing is a narrow mean looking street opening at the top into a handsome though small square, where the chancellor of the exchequer and the prime minister reside.

The chancellor of the exchequer, Mr. Bonar Law, resides in the adjoining house, No. 11. I don't just remember whether he is a "Sir" yet or not. I did not know that he lived next door until I reached the place and saw a "Bobbie"—a cop—standing there, and I engaged him in conversation and he gave me this story.

The building was first put up in 1735, and has been used continually for prime ministers. From the outside, it is a very ordinary looking building. But on the inside it is finely furnished.

It has a large brass plate on the front door and three highly polished doorbells with large brass rings. There are thirteen windows about fourteen inches wide and ten inches wide with common glass windowpanes. I thought to myself that it was a poor looking place from the outside.

The officer says they are on guard there all the time, changing every few hours. Then I asked who lives next door and he told me Mr. Bonar Law. Then I looked again.

I talked with the officer from 2:00 p.m. until 3:10 p.m. After which, two sailors came up and began to talk over the same thing. They wanted to see where Lloyd George lived and they asked questions. From what they asked, I got considerable information without having to ask myself.

They were British sailors and could say what they liked. They spoke right out and said they thought little of the place, etc. The officer was very pleasant with me after they left. They talked possibly a half hour.

A detective then came up. I saw his badge under his coat and we all three talked. I soon got around to the point and let them know who I was and what I was doing, only looking over the city between hours. They seemed to be interested in me and told me some few things.

Two young ladies came out of the Mr. George home.

I asked if they were his daughters. The cop said, "No," and that they were visitors. I thought by staying and talking there was the possibility that Lloyd George might incidentally come to the window or door to take a look out but there was nothing doing, so I left for a ball game between the US and the pennant winners of Canada at Stamford Bridge.

Wednesday evening, October 9th, Commander McBride gave a dinner at 14 Great Cumberland Place in honor of Commander LeBritton of the Navy. Those present: Commander McBride, Commander Higgins, Commander LeBritton, Commander Land, Colonel Kennedy, Captain Franklin.

And as things are running my way, I had the honor of waiting the dinner, which just suited me, not just exactly wishing anyone any bad luck. But I would not care if someone took sick every time there was a dinner. Well, Commander Higgins was elected to make up a Navy cocktail, and I found out the difference between that and the Bronx cocktail that Mr. I. C. Elder and T. B. Kennedy showed me how to make. This is the one that I make. They said it makes you sit up a little straighter.

Commander Higgins's cocktails were very satisfactory and were very much enjoyed.

At the dinner, there were some very amusing incidents told of how we are making the kaiser yell. Commander LeBritton told of just how long it takes a 20,000-ton ship to go down. He is very anxious to take a trip to New York. Commander McBride is very much interested as to when they will get that ship off the rocks that went on some days ago. He asked this information of Captain Franklin. Commander Higgins says that is just what he wants to know. Commander McBride said he is sure there is a box with five hundred Pall Mall cigarettes in the ship for him. And Commander Higgins says the ship has two letters on for him. I also noticed that the colonel was very much interested in this talk as no letters from Ragged Edge have arrived for some time, and he told me if some did not come soon he was going to take someone else's letters.

Captain Franklin finally said that he was or rather felt sure that there would be nothing saved from that boat.

The dinner was a complete success and all present had a very pleasant evening. The table was laden with everything that was wanted to make one eat. If the appetite was not strong, the things were there to repair it.

For some time Colonel Kennedy has been trying to locate First Lieutenant King Alexander, of Chambersburg, PA. He has now been successful in locating him at the hospital at Portsmouth. He has phoned him and asked him to come to London as soon as he can conveniently do so and spend some time with him. On Thursday, October 10, Lieutenant Alexander came to London, arriving Victoria Station at 12:08 p.m.

I was there to meet him and take him to the office, where he had a good chat with the staff while waiting on the colonel to finish a meeting. He has certainly been right in the thick of the fighting. He has lost two fingers off his left hand and he said he did not know that there was shrapnel in them until the nurse was massaging the hand, found something hard, and the doctor then used an X-ray and found it there. He carries it as a souvenir. He looks fairly well. I think he is just a trifle shell-shocked. The doctor told him he would let him go home if he wanted to, but he has the nerve and says he thinks he would like to stay and see the finish. That shows the kind of spirit he has. It also shows that he is game all the way through. No yellow about him.

The colonel took him to the Officer's Club for dinner and to a show tonight, called "As You Were." It is considered one of the finest shows that ever hit London. First Lieutenant Alexander has been gassed in the knee with what is called the mustard gas. It burns and is very severe. He got his last wound at Chateau Thierry and has just been relieved by the Scotch Guard. He waited to see that they understood what their duty was and that all was right, before leaving for the hospital. He looks more like his father now than ever. He is a real picture of him. Even talks like his father. Chief Clerk Houser and Sergeant Smith had him looking over the map of the fighting area, and it is very, very interesting to hear him go over the ground. He knows it all. Can go from one battleground to another. He says there are about two thousand cases in the Portsmouth Hospital and they expect to have about four thousand in all. The hospital already now has cots in the halls and that they are bringing more from St. Quentin and Cambria in about three days time.

Colonel Kennedy has certainly done many kind and fatherly acts toward many young men in the service. In many particular cases that were very touching.

Last Monday the eighth of October, they opened at Trafalgar Square a War Bond Campaign. The main idea was to feed the guns with and by buying War Bonds.

A beautiful lady by the name of Miss Taylor recited a poem on [why there was a need to] feed the guns. On the Monument of Nelson they had a large screen that they showed a movie of the airships, how the vessels are made, the speed that is used, the submarines in action, bombing towns in Germany, and many other things that entered into the operation of the war. I was there several nights and saw many things that were new to me.

The papers are full of the news that Germany has laid down. It has put me out of the writing humor this morning. The colonel has gone to Woburn Sands to spend the day. I want to get all over London, as I fear that home spirit will hit some places and my experience with the locals will change. I had hope of reaching Berlin, but I now fear I am doomed.

Royal A. Christian observed large crowds gathering at Trafalgar Square in London right before and after Germany's signing of the Armistice on November 11, 1918. This photograph, taken two days prior, captures the Lord Mayor's procession, with the Church of St. Martin in the Fields in the background. Courtesy of the National Archives and Records Administration, College Park, Maryland, 38403[250D8]

On March 12, 1918, the all-black 369th Regiment was assigned to the French Army as replacement troops. It was one of four infantry regiments from the 93rd Division to serve with the French for the remainder of the war. At the conclusion of the war, the entire 369th regiment was awarded France's highest honor for bravery, the Croix de Guerre. Author's collection

Houser and Smith and Mackenson have had a great time kidding me about going home this morning.

Belgrave Mansion Hotel, the headquarters of AEF, has a frontage on Grovernor Garden about four hundred feet, runs back to Ebury Mews about two hundred feet to Buckingham Palace Road, two hundred feet on Ebury Street and two hundred feet on Buckingham Palace Road. It has one hundred ninety rooms; the entire building is used for the American Army AEF headquarters. The Gorman Hotel on Ebury Street has about ninety rooms and is in the rear of the Belgrave Hotel. It is used for Post Office and offices of the AEF.

It is amusing; the English people here are after a holiday every few days. They come into the office and ask Mr. Houser if such a day is a holiday in the building. It seems that these people here have many days that are not considered holidays in the States. As this office is the head of things, they always ask here. In the morning, I often hear Captain Franklin and Colonel Kennedy and Commander [Higgins] kidding in the bathroom about the one-hundred-year war. Well, I think it would have taken that long for these people to beat Germany had not the US come in to help them the way they go at it.

The *Leinster* was sunk by a submarine last week. It was a hard blow to this office. Captain Cone, who was well known to all in this office and a great, close personal friend to Colonel Kennedy, was on the boat. Reports say he had both legs broken in the smash and that he is now in the hospital at Dublin.

He has dined at 14 Great Cumberland Place many times and was the right hand bar to Admiral Sims, the conqueror of the U-boat.

With General Pershing these are the people that brought Germany to her knees.

And one would be surprised to know that the people on this side do not care to give General Pershing much credit for it. Very little is said of him in the papers over here. There seems to be a great deal of jealousy at the bottom. I guess I will leave that alone. I may be going too deep.

In a conversation with France a few moments ago, Mr. Houser told them that Germany had thrown up their hands. They had not heard the news over there yet and were very much surprised to hear it. The telephone is very clear this morning and this being the thirteenth day, I guess that accounts for everything that has happened.

I went with the band to Buckingham Palace this morning, saw the guards change, and then to St. James Palace to hear them play three selections and drill.

If I had anything to do with it, Colonel Kennedy would be placed on the committee that goes to Germany to sign the peace terms.

I also have a little thought that the friends that Colonel Kennedy has made in England are so many that I think it might be necessary for him to visit London with his family, later.

On Sunday afternoon, October 13th, I went to see the Victoria and Albert Museum at South Kensington. All in all, there is too much, cause I cannot describe all that I saw properly.

I then went to the British Museum and looked that over and I was just about as much puzzled there as in the other one.

I saw many of the old ancient carriages used by the kings and queens in the fifteenth century, and the sedan chairs that great rulers were carried in during those times. There were many paintings from the Holy Lands that I thought I would see. But things look blue now.

There was a large statue of "David" cut from a solid piece of marble by a great Italian sculptor, and several stone fountains from the Holy Lands. Three of the fountains were about four feet deep, solid marble and about three feet round.

All kinds of Persian carpets are displayed and are especially fine. There are several very large tapestries, and Italian and French furniture.

The collection of animals is hard to excel. Seal, bear, mountain lion, and every kind of animal ever heard of is there.

When I first attempted to come over here, there was quite a dispute between Mr. Logue and Mr. F. W. Hankins as to who could get me off properly. Finally, it was Mr. Logue. On the first attempt, we could not get through. Well, Mr. Hankins had a laugh on us and he had it in his mind that he could have succeeded had it been left to him. There were some things that came up that we could not overcome. And while I speak it very quietly, I hardly think that he could have either; nevertheless, the last time Mr. Logue went after it, he came through one hundred percent, and I landed here.

Mr. Hankins, just before I left, whispered to me that he would soon be with me and would meet me at Leicester Square. I have located the square and know it very well, but just a few weeks ago word came over that Major F. W. Hankins cannot get over. The Washington powers that be, the same powers that stopped me, say he is needed there and refuse him passports. While it shows the value of the services of the master mechanic of the CVRR, it at the same time stops one who we all would like to have here with us.

Now, I am really very sorry for him, as I know he wanted to get away from the States, and if I was not so far from him I would suggest that he see Mr. H. A. Logue. Maybe he could land him on this side.

Mr. Hankins is certainly a popular official, well liked by the entire force, and one of those sort who is always in good humor. He has taught me a whole lot about private cars, which are not doing very much work just now.

Time will change all things. In due time the colonel will get back to the states and help to keep the force busy. His monthly letter he sends from the states is eagerly looked for and every word is read.

On Tuesday evening, October 15th, Colonel Kennedy entertained First Lieutenant G. E. Williams, Field Clerk A. G. Houser, and Sergeant Warren E. Smith, at 14 Great Cumberland Place, and then presented them with tickets to see "As You Were" at the theater.

I noticed that day there was an unusual stir and people seemed very happy, and that the show was such a rage. I thought something was stirring, and later in the day I got wise.

Well, the next day I think Smith could have taken five hundred words a minute. He felt so good, and Chief Clerk Houser was dictating as clear as a bell.

About two weeks ago, I was at the post office in the Goring Hotel for the mail. I got a package for Sergeant Warren E. Smith. It was not so heavy nor so large. I was ordered to open it, which I was happy to do and it contained a two-pound box of caramel candy, one pound of crystalized ginger—just to think of it, crystalized ginger—and one dozen cakes of chocolate. Well, I always did like them fellows, but just now I over-liked. I just picked Smith up and loved him.

And Houser helped him to take a record of it while I helped him eat. The package came from a Mrs. Ryan of New York City. I hope that lady will live forever and I certainly hope she will soon send another package. It was real candy, and the ginger I looked at for a long time; so long since I saw any and the taste was—oh, it was all there.

Houser suggested to Smith that it might last longer if it was kept in his drawer under lock and key, but I said it was hardly worthwhile to do that, that the idea of this war is to teach men to act as brothers toward each other and share with your fellow man, etc.

One of Royal A. Christian's duties was to pick up and send mail from the Goring Hotel on Ebury Street in London. The hotel also served as the headquarters for the United States Signal Corps, which was responsible for communicating the war as it unfolded. Through photography, print publications, and film, the Signal Corps documented the theater of war from an American standpoint. Courtesy of the National Archives and Records Administration, College Park, Maryland, 25341[1095T8]

Well, tonight brings up another story that Germany has surrendered and that Turkey has caused it. Last night there was an awful mob of people on the streets walking and running up White Hall to Parliament Street to Lloyd George's house, calling for speeches, etc.

I have looked very carefully and talked to the many colored soldiers as to how and what they were doing to help the cause. I find that they have done wonderful work, they have unloaded the largest liners that float in from one to two days, when heretofore it took weeks to do it, and in the railroad work as laying track and unloading cars they work and beat all records, assisting in the mechanical work of the army trucks. They have been right on the job.

The English people do not look down on the colored man as in America, and as long as you behave yourself you are treated all right.

Part of the Signal Corps operations at the Goring Hotel, the office of telegraph and telephone maintained lines of communication with the American forces in France and officials in the United States. This office was extremely important to the transportation department and its efforts to maintain the constant movement of supplies and troops to the front. Courtesy of the National Archives and Record Administration, College Park, Maryland, 29533[2080T8]

You are served in any restaurant or cafe or barbershop in London, no color line is drawn.

Of course, some funny things will happen to all nations at times. Monday, October 14th, I went to Victoria Station to get the evening paper. I saw two colored soldiers talking together. I said "Hello" and went up to them. We talked for a few minutes. I saw the one fellow watching a lady pretty strong, and she was flirting with him. I thought it was my move and left. Going across the street I looked back. He went to the lady (white) and they talked, he walked away with her. She took him by the arm.

On the corner of our headquarters a man stands with flowers every day. I came from the station so I would pass them again, and just as they passed the lady said something about pretty flowers. Down in his pockets the boy went. I said, "I bet he buys her red flowers." And he did, he got her a big bunch of red roses. She put them on her breast and up the street they went a short distance when a taxi passed. The driver was wise (Reuben was in town) and he yelled "Cab." The sport said, "Yes, come on, let's ride." And in they got. Now you can imagine the sight. A real black man, white woman, red roses. Well, we have often heard it said—"Fool and money soon part."

Talking to an Australian soldier today, he was telling me his troubles. He stopped at the Maple Leaf Club; someone stole his shoes and $25. He did not know the person that took them, but he sure did say things about him. It is mean the way they steal from the soldiers at these places.

I had never bothered any of the YMCA huts or clubs over here. They are "for uniformed men only." No matter, I wanted to see the city—and such sights. However, it is now getting cool and I must find some inside place to continue to get more information about the city.

Field Clerk Houser and Sergeant Smith have been telling me from time to time that I could get in to the huts. So Friday evening I went to the Eagle Hut. I was satisfied I had papers and credentials enough to get into any place. Well, I asked for the manager and we had a talk. I showed him my papers and he said, "O.K. You can come in any time you want." Well, I looked over the place. It is very clean and seems to be properly kept up. There is quite a crowd there and the order is, well, I guess pretty good.

There are so many huts around the city; I hardly think I will spend much time in any one. Then again, I am kept fairly busy in the evenings a little too late for the shows.

The Eagle Hut is maintained by the Americans, but is used by all soldiers. They have shower baths, two pool tables, one pocket billiard table, three pianos, and an auditorium for shows. They have shows every night. They have also bedrooms for the boys from the front, so they can be taken care of.

As the song goes, it is always fair weather when good fellows get together and a good song's ringing clear.

Only soft drinks are sold in the place. However, but there was some evidence that something had been gotten on the outside, from the appearance of a few soldiers.

On the piano, I played "Hail, hail, the gang's all here" and "We won't get back till it's over, over here," and the boys began to sing and I felt very much at home.

As those are the only tunes that I thought I could play with any degree of time, I did not attempt any others.

They had lady attendants and they all seem to have enough to do. The club closes at twelve every night. Beds are reserved until 9:30.

Prices are what they call fair. The cheapest cigar is 7d, which in our money is fourteen cents. You can be sure, I did not need many at that price.

On Thursday evening, October 17th, Colonel Kennedy went to Earlwood Surrey to spend the night with Mr. Sanderson. It is about twenty miles from London, on the London, Brighton & South Coast Ry. He was due back Friday morning at 9:08 a.m., but on account of heavy fog the train was thirty minutes late. The fog on Friday morning was the worst I ever saw and the other people say the same. Truly, you could just barely see the house on the far side of the street.

At the Victoria Station when I went to see the colonel, I saw a large bulletin board saying that trains would run late, due to the fog, and so many trains would be taken off. That is what they do in foggy weather here.

At the stations here, the tickets are about one and one-half inches by two and one-half inches. If you want to go through the gates to see friends off, or to meet someone, you must pay 1d, and you get a ticket. They also use machines like the ones we have in the States to get chewing gum out of, to purchase a ticket. You deposit a penny and a ticket will drop out.

You can also get tickets to many places on the underground the same way. It does away with crowds gathering, but even at that there are so many people here that it is really nothing to see as many as fifty lined up at the ticket window.

The conditions for riding the train on the back of the ticket are that the company will not be responsible for any accident that occurs and explains that the ticket must be given up at the gate and is not transferable, etc.

The effect of the fog is very bad on the throat and lungs. They have lady gate attendants at the stations. I tried to get the rate of pay, and her duties from one of these attendants, while waiting for the colonel. She said they work eight hours a day and that they do not receive the same rate of pay as the men who did the same work. She said their pay is a little better now than it was, but I could not get her to say the amount. She also said the women in the munitions plants and conductresses of the trams get the same rate as men. I said, "Well, the railroads are owned by the government, are they not?" She said, "Yes, but they take jolly good care of the money and will not pay us as they did the men."

Saturday evening, October 19th, Lieutenant Commander John S. Higgins gave a dinner at 14 Great Cumberland Place for and in honor of the Lord of the American Navy in England, and the conqueror of U-boats, Admiral W. S. Sims.

Well, the table was all fixed for the occasion and everything was in apple pie order, and at 7:57 p.m. the bell rang, and I opened the door for this wonderful American, who will go down in history as the greatest ever to enter.

Well, when he came in, I don't think I was walking any place but in the air. I certainly was proud to be able to wait on such a great man.

The Navy officers all wear beautiful large capes. You should have seen how tenderly I assisted the Hon. Sir with his cape and he is one of the, Oh, well, I cannot express it. I asked him up to the living room and Lieutenant Commander Higgins met him at the head of the stairs. For the rest of the evening I was about as happy as I think I would have been if I was in Berlin.

Commander Higgins shook his hand and turned him over to Colonel Kennedy, who did the chatting. Navy Constructor L. B. McBride, who assists the admiral to sink the U-boats arrived and is followed by Commander Higgins who has made up the appetizing Navy cocktails. They all drank to the health of Admiral Sims.

Then they marched down to the table and the feed was on, with everybody on their toes, particularly Roy. Captain Franklin told of the Embarkation of soldiers. Commander LeBritton, brother-in-law of Mr. McBride, had all his wit with him.

Well, things were going from then on—port wine and possibly some things a little stronger were served.

Those present: Admiral W. S. Sims, Colonel M. C. Kennedy, Captain W. S. Franklin, Commander LeBritton, Constructor McBride, Lieutenant Commander John S. Higgins.

As the news continued to come in good from the front, it is hard to tell how many more of these dinners will be pulled off.

This is Sunday, October 20th, and I just came from the St. Martins-in-the-Fields services. It was awful nice. The band played very nicely and the singing was fine.

They have no choir. The entire audience does the singing. The minister spoke very nicely and only for twenty minutes. He said that after this war is over the great question will be "Is religion any good or not. If good, accept it—if bad, reject it." But at any decision you arrive at, do not decide until you have given it the consideration that is justly due it.

And he said the day is fast coming when there will be only one church. And that some people will not want to believe, but he claims we will all see it. He says we can all get this religion, but that it is thundering hard to live in this world and keep it.

There were sixteen ushers lifting the collected and all met in the center aisle and marched to the rostrum, where they are met by some head usher who had a large tray. All the money was deposited on this tray. It seemed to be pretty heavy. The collection was very good. They marched right past where I was sitting. I could easily see the size of the baskets. They were pretty well filled. They had some silver pieces in, too; they were not all pennies.

I judge the church would hold possibly fifteen hundred or more. They have a balcony all the way around that was well filled at today's services.

They opened at 3:00 p.m. and are supposed to start at 3:30 p.m., but they were five minutes late today.

Everyone left out promptly at 4:45 p.m. The minister speaks very plainly and you can hear him very distinctly.

The hymns played by this band were well known to everyone and I tell you, the church rang. When they sing their national hymn, it can be heard for a long distance.

I was anxious to write this up right away, as the colonel told me I need not show up at the house this evening. I am going to Westminster Abbey. Well, two celebrated churches like that in one day is "going some" for a small town boy.

Well, I have been to the Westminster Abbey and heard the sermon, and now feel I have put in a pretty good day of church.

The Right Reverend Rennie MacInnes preached tonight. He is the bishop in Jerusalem and he is just a little bit long-winded. He preached for forty minutes.

It was real interesting though. He told about the Turks and how the British came to their rescue, and how the British saved Palestine. He talked about how the River Jordan's water was bad. He was a pretty good speaker.

That is about all I can remember of the sermon. It seems I cannot keep them in my mind very long.

This has been a fearful, ugly, rainy day. It has kept it up all day, but there was a very large crowd at both churches today. The abbey had a very large turnout tonight.

The abbey opens the doors at 6:00 p.m. and begins services at 6:30 p.m. sharp. The minister preached forty minutes and dismissed everyone at 8:00 p.m. One can hardly kick on that time.

The choir was right up to the mark. That organ is surely a sweet-toned instrument.

This morning while I was putting on Colonel Kennedy's puttees, Captain Franklin said, "Colonel, I had a dream about you last night." The colonel said, "What was it?" The captain said, "I dreamed that General Pershing, you, and I were at dinner and that General Pershing put you in charge of the embarkation." The colonel said, "Was the war over?" "No," said Captain Franklin. "Well," the colonel said, "where was I going to embark to?" The captain said that part did not come out in the dream. The colonel said, "The only place I want to embark to is Chambersburg."

Well, today, October 24th, Colonel Kennedy went to Dover, England, to inspect some railroads, and he told me I could go to London Tower. Now, I did not need any second telling. Chief Clerk Houser said I had been a good messenger and I could skip at noon. Well, I sure did go some this day. Took the Tube at Victoria Station for London Tower.

Bloody Tower: This tower dates from the reign of Edward III and Richard II, and was called by its present name as early as 1597. It was originally known as the Garden Tower and was popularly believed to be the scene of the murder of Edward V and his brother, the Duke of York, as well as Henry VI.

The execution block and axe are in the White Tower. The axe has been in the tower since 1687 and it is certainly an odd looking article. It sets right in front of the cell that Sir Walter Raleigh once occupied. As for the block, it looks like you lay your breast up against the larger side of the block and your chin is supposed to rest on the other side, leaving your neck on the top of the block. It has evidently played its part in its time, and as I like to get souvenirs of things, this is one of the things that I do not want any part of.

In this tower, Sir Walter Raleigh spent about twelve years of his life as a prisoner. Raleigh's Walk is the walk along which he was allowed to exercise. Here is where he wrote his History of the World.

In the Chapel of St. Peter-ad-Vincula, beneath the altar lie the remains of Anne Boleyn, Katherine Howard, Lady Jane Grey, the Duke of Monmouth, and many others beheaded in the Tower.

In those days when they took a prisoner to the court to be tried, they hauled him or her, as the case may be, in a wagon and they had the axe pointed away from the prisoner. On their return if you were found guilty, as most always happened, the axe was pointed at you.

One thing you can be sure of, that the sins did not all originate in Chambersburg, for from what I have seen on this side the sins over here are something awful.

Among some of the other things I saw at the tower was what is called "Bilboe." It is an instrument used on people to make them confess. You are laid down, a band is put around your neck and one around each hand; then another goes around each ankle, then there is a sort of a handle to it, and that is pulled back and forth until all slack is taken out. And, then it begins to pinch you. Arms pulled out straight, the neck will be pulled up and feet pulled down. After you are howling with pain, they ask you if you are ready to confess, and they will leave you in that position for some time. Then if you do not confess, they will put you back in a cell and in several days they will give you the dose over again. As the guard said, a man or woman would confess that the moon was right in his pocket or any other thing, rather than go through this ordeal again.

The shields and armor worn by the fighters in the twelfth and thirteenth centuries are also shown and are certainly kept in good condition. They had a shield that covered the horse, as well as the man. As for weight, a horse had to carry about four hundred pounds.

On my way back from the Tower, I got off the train at Westminster Station and went over to the Westminster Abbey and joined a party there that was being shown through parts of the church that you are not allowed to see on Sunday.

The Abbey was started in about the eleventh century and they have been adding to it ever since. When the war first started, a bomb hit the church. It happened not to be a very good one and did not do too much damage. It hit near the chair that the kings and queens have been crowned in and broke several pieces off of the walls and statutes nearby, but did not damage the chair.

The graves in which all the kings and queens are buried are covered with large bags of sand, and from what the guide says, there must be nearly as many people buried in Westminster Abbey as there are killed in this war.

Oliver Cromwell, who was very much against the church, tried to destroy as much of it as possible. Several angels have their heads broken off, and several statues have been disfigured by him and his band of followers. Yet he left a dying request to be buried in the church, and his wishes were carried out.

The guide that was with the party held some exalted place in the church. I don't remember what he said it was now, but he certainly knew the church like a book. He said many of the people who have been buried at the church were common and no account classes, but they were connected with people that did have money and they paid to have them buried there.

Booth and Barrett, both wonderful actors in their time, are buried in the Abbey near the statue of Shakespeare. The guide said that the Germans say Shakespeare was a German. I wonder what Shakespeare would say if he could hear that now.

Now, aside from the kings and queens, nearly all the people are buried in the floor, or ground rather, and brass letters at their head saying who they are, their birth and death, etc.

The kings and queens they all have some large sort of a tomb, like an altar, with all kinds of fancy marble cut around and a likeness of what the person would look like in real life.

The Dark Cloister is where the monks lived while in the abbey. It is worn down on one side very much, now they do not allow you to walk on that side. As it was a sort of double-gate affair, you must walk on the other side. The marble step shows that a great deal of walking on it has been done.

You also find that the Tower of London and Westminster Abbey go hand in hand in many ways. In terms of both of crime and good deeds, as many of the things that happened in the abbey were settled in the Tower.

In one of the first parts of the abbey to be built, there is a long seat where the Pilgrims sat waiting on the abbot to pass; as he did every morning there was church. He always gave them a shilling. The guide says that the shilling he gave them at that time was worth ten times the kind we have now. And he also gave them a hunk of cheese and a bowl of ale. The guide said that if that was done now, he would be there every damn morning himself.

It costs 6d, in our money twelve cents, to go through. It is, without a doubt, the most interesting place I think a person should see. You could never write enough about it, and you could never remember all you see. It has so many holes and corners—some very dark and some well lighted.

The Poets Corner is very interesting to see, as England had some good poets and writers.

One also finds that many of these kings and queens here were not spotless when it came to crime either. It seems they did their share of the bad deeds, too.

You find that most of the guides that carry you around in these places will more or less make a few little hints for a small amount. In other words, I have never seen people like tips more than here in England. The Englishman is easily bribed. If you want anything, a shilling will come near turning the trick.

And, if you want to know anything and your time is short, my experience has been that you must pay for it. It may be a little expensive but you get the information and that is what you are after.

Saturday morning, October 26th, on opening the mail, there was a letter from Miss Mary Sharpe, of Chambersburg, PA, saying she had arrived in London, and was stopping at the Imperial Hotel.

The colonel said, "Roy, get her on the phone at once." After several efforts it was found she had left. Finally, she called at 1:15 p.m. and the colonel called to see her at 7:45 p.m. on Saturday, as did also Chief Clerk A. G. Houser. She very kindly asked for Roy and the colonel told me to go to see her Sunday at about 1:00 p.m. I went to the hotel shortly after 1:00 p.m., and found that the lady had gone to Westminster Abbey. So I just planted myself and waited. A little after 2 p.m. she came in. Well, when I saw her coming in the door I really—well, I felt good at the sight of one from the good old "Burg."

I spoke to her and she shook hands and said she was glad to see me. I could tell she was by her expression. And, while I did not just exactly want her to know how I was going to write her up, she was pretty wise.

When I said, "What boat did you come over on," at once she very quietly told me the *Anchises*. I at once knew she was wise.

She left Chambersburg on October 6th, for New York and went aboard the ship *Anchises* on Friday, October 11th. The ship steamed out from the pier Saturday, October 12th, and laid in the river all night, and setting sail for this side on Sunday, October 13th. There were eleven ships in the convoy and one battleship, one cruiser and the regular bunch of destroyers that follow up the convoys until they are well out of the harbor.

She spoke of the sight of the airships that followed the convoy. It really is a wonderful sight. They had fine weather all the way over. She had a very pleasant roommate. As the staterooms are not very large, she was fortunate enough to have only a suitcase, while her friend had a small trunk. As both were very healthy, they got through the trip without getting sick. The cooking is something that people from our good Valley will never get used to. Taking things as they come, she being used to plenty of meat, did not mind the English cooking that used no salt, less pepper, and forget the butter in the seasoning of all vegetables. She made the best of things and we sure were glad to see her.

I asked her if she saw any subs. She said no, she did not, but some of those on board the ship said they saw one. The ship she was on was the second in the convoy, and Miss Mary was of the opinion it was in a good place, safe from the subs. She found out later, from the crew, that it was in the most dangerous part of the convoy. It is good she did not know that, for it might have worried her all the way over. You see a sub hitting or shooting for the leading ship; the second one is very likely to catch the blow.

She made it across and then about five days from Liverpool the rudder went bad on her ship and it pulled away from the convoy for several hours. Toward evening she came into line again, the rudder having been repaired. Then all went well until they were about the coast of Ireland, when one of the ships spotted a mine. Luckily, for that ship, it saw the mine fairly quickly and, it being a very foggy night, the ships were compelled to signal the entire night to keep from running together. It was a very dangerous thing to do, for the subs can get onto their course.

They got through there all right without any further trouble and docked at Liverpool on Thursday, October 24th, where they spent the night before coming to London, Friday afternoon. When she wrote Colonel Kennedy, the letter coming to headquarters Saturday morning and he was able to see her Saturday evening. She is on her way to France, not able to say yet just what place she will be sent. She is also not sure just when she will sail from London. The going on these trips is done without very much advance information—it is a case of being always ready.

Miss Sharpe said there was not much sickness on the ship she was on. I am glad to hear of that, because some of them that came in here were certainly loaded down with sick cases and many were buried at sea.

She looks awful well in her natty uniform and reports everything is in bad shape at home in the way of "Flu." Well, there is plenty of that over here, and if you want to make someone run, just cough or sneeze and you will have plenty of room.

She was also in the "Eagle Hut" on Friday night, and as she says the work of the Red Cross, in which she is engaged, is chiefly to keep the boys in good humor. Well, that is true and right. If the soldier boys that Miss Mary Sharpe comes in contact with knew of her fine qualities, beautiful ladyship, and standing in the community of Chambersburg, as I do, God knows they would get in good humor and stay in good humor until her mother said "Yes."

After talking for some time, she said, "Roy, I have nothing much to give you" (and you know I was not expecting anything), "but if you will excuse me for a minute, I have some fruitcake. I will give it to you and you can give Colonel Kennedy some. Now, wait right here." Now, "wait" was my middle name. She was only gone a few moments when she returned with a tin box of fruitcake. Well, this colonel of mine is a dandy—he gets me many good things.

You see, I will offer the fruitcake to him. He won't eat much sweet and over it will come to Roy. Of course, if the title was any lower than colonel, well, I will offer him the fruitcake. But won't that taste good from the old burg? Miss Mary has her twenty pounds of sugar allowed each passenger into this country. I do not think she will have any trouble with it in entering France, or this would have been the proper place to unload for the 14 Great Cumberland Place mess can use sugar from that good old town.

There were about 35,000 soldiers on the convoy she was on, and I truly hope she will get over to France all right and when the fuss is over that she will get home safely. I am sure she will be very much surprised when she reads the few lines that I have put here.

The 806th Pioneer Infantry Band was organized at Camp Funston, Kansas, in July 1918, and arrived in France two months later. As a labor battalion first, the 806th performed all the expected duties from building bridges and roads to unloading supplies destined for the front. As a regimental band, the 806th entertained servicemen and civilians throughout France, playing both military standards and jazz. This photograph was taken at Leoville, France. Author's collection

On Monday, October 28th, the Japanese Prince [arrived in] London to visit the king. I was sent up to Bond Street to get some tickets to a Red Cross Ball that was to be held that night. As I saw a very large crowd on Piccadilly, near the Admiralty Arch, where you go to Buckingham Palace, I was told they were watching for the prince and the king. I went on the errand and on my way back I went through St. James Park and passed the palace, and there was the prince and the entire staff.

The band was with the party. Two airships were in the air and the squadron of Police was around the party. They were driven to Hotel Rubins, which faces the Royal Stables on Buckingham Palace Road.

The prince stays with the king in the palace, while his staff and aide-de-camps and servants, in all consisting of fourteen persons, went into Hotel Rubins. As soon as the party went into the hotel, the Japanese Flag was run up the pole on top of the hotel. And that will stay there until the party leaves; that I am told is the way the royal families visit each other. It sure is some expense to the State to carry a party of that size.

They are certainly on the job when it comes to guarding the royal families. The secret service men all wear long blue coats with a blue striped band on the left arm. They also have a very large guard of mounted men as well as autos. It would be a very hard job to try to injure any of them and get away.

Nearly every night during the week they have a show at Eagle Hut. On Sundays, they have a minister speak to the boys.

On Thursday night, October 31st, I was there and they had a show and it was very interesting. After an act or so, the jazz band played and the soldiers danced and the girls danced. But there is an order that prevents the boys and girls dancing together in the canteens.

So the boys dance alone and the girls dance alone and all seem pretty happy. After the dancing, the floor manager has some games that makes more fun.

He calls for eight boys and they come in a hurry up in front of the stage, then he calls for eight girls and they come; now he will have a wheelbarrow race. The boys get down on their hands and the girls hold their feet in the air like wheel-barrow handles and they are to run on their hands about twenty-five feet, turn and come back. Usually some fall down, sometimes the girls fall down, and it will sure put everybody in good humor to see them at it.

Then a lady will play a violin solo, followed by the quartette singing some of the popular songs, and then the jazz band will hit up some of the rag time stuff that will make you forget your mother.

The floor manager will call for ten boys again, then ten girls, and he will have what they call a fishing party. Now the ten girls will get up on the stage and each will have a stick about four feet long and on the end securely tie an apple. Then he gets ten more girls and one stands behind and holds the hands of each boy, and he is to catch the apple in his mouth. Well such twisting to get hold of the apple you never saw. Those that get the apples are paired up with the girl that held the apple. This makes more fun for the audience. As I get it from one of the staff in charge, the idea is to keep the boys in good humor, and because some of the girls are from good families, they did not want them to think they must dance with soldiers. Of course, at public dances there is nothing to prohibit them from dancing with who they please.

On the evening I speak of, there was a very pretty Scotch Lassie who sang for the boys. She had been singing through the US in the interest of Liberty Bonds, and she was really pretty and had a lovely voice. Now know this, a good singer is generally very popular with the boys anyhow, but she was pretty with it. That calls for more talk. Well, this lady sang "Blue Bells of Scotland," "Auld Lang Syne," and "Star Spangled Banner," and it was fine. After the show was over, I was walking quietly around. When I looked to the left, there was Field Clerk Houser and Sergeant Warren E. Smith with this Scotch lassie. She had a beautiful head of hair of the blonde variety and pretty white teeth, and a large plaid dress with a sort of a throw over her shoulders. The Scotch people wear a sort of kilt that hangs in front of them. From what I understand, it is made out of the hair of different kinds of animals. Well, she had one of them and it was white, and with the large white and black plaid dress she had on it made her look very chic.

They did not see me. I eased away and I spoke of it lightly the next morning. Sergeant Smith was very anxious to know where I was. I do not think I have ever seen him more interested than right down there. He was busy telling this Scotch lassie what the Flagler System goes through, the fine country, and so on.

I fear Houser did not get in much about the Cumberland Valley, and possibly it may not suit her to come this way, for I really believe Smith *might* try to stop her in New York.

The ladies that work in the YMCAs here all wear a black and white striped gingham dress, with a black collar on it, and it makes them all look in harmony with one another.

I was walking around in the Eagle Hut on Saturday night, October 26th, when I saw a face that looked very familiar. He looked at me and I at him, and then he said, "Where have I seen you?" I thought of New York, of the PRR, and then he said he was with the Bellevue-Stratford, Philadelphia, and then I knew. He was the assistant manager, Mr. Lorentz Maresch. He was with the Red Cross and came in the same convoy as Miss Mary Sharpe. He called Sunday on Colonel Kennedy, whom he knew very well.

On Wednesday evening, October 30th, Colonel Kennedy gave a dinner at 14 Great Cumberland Place in honor of Colonel W. J. Wilgus, of Tours, France.

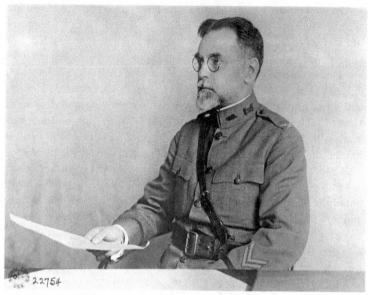

Colonel William J. Wilgus, deputy director general of transportation for the US Army, in his office at Ranne's Barracks in Tours, France, in August 1918. His uniform bears two six-month chevrons on the left sleeve. The former vice president of the New York Central Railroad, Wilgus secured enlistments of railroad men for service as officers in the railway regiments overseas. Courtesy of the National Archives and Records Administration, College Park, Maryland, 22754[1524G8]

Well I have heard so much of Colonel Wilgus that I have really all along felt I knew him.

He was in the United States several months ago. He tried to take me back with him to England to turn me over later to Colonel Kennedy. When I went into the room with Colonel Wentz's handsome gift to the colonel, having filled it with ice, and starting to shake things just up before dinner, Colonel Wilgus said, "Why there is Roy. Roy, I have heard lots of you and I certainly wanted to bring you along over with me, but the Powers That Be prevented me from doing so. I guess I did not have pull enough." Of course, I thanked him for what he did do and I thought it very kind of him, but when Captain Franklin's brother, who owns the whole steamship line from New York to Europe, got through the Powers That Be fell back.

Those present: Colonel M. C. Kennedy, Colonel W. J. Wilgus, Colonel D. B. Wentz, Captain W. S. Franklin, Commander J. S. Higgins, Mr. Jackson, in charge of food stock.

Well, there was a very pleasant evening spent at the mess. Everyone was very sorry that it was impossible for Navy Constructor L. B. McBride to be present, as he had expected to be, but everyone that is in touch knows he is the happiest man now that he has the kaiser's submarines beaten to a frazzle. We also know that he is very anxious to get back to the States to Mrs. McBride, so he has to miss the parties to figure a little closer for Kaiser Bill.

Of course during all these days of battling the kaiser, and while there are many people who think that it was all pleasure here, some have suffered a great many things that are not known.

Since being over here, Lieutenant Colonel D. B. Wentz has lost his father, Colonel W. J. Wilgus lost his wife, and Colonel Kennedy lost his brother-in-law, Mr. I. C. Elder.

So, you can see it is pretty hard when you lose friends that are so close to you. Being so far away, you cannot get to them while they are sick, nor attend the last services over them.

Colonel Wentz leaves here Friday for Cardiff, Wales, and will be back again Sunday. He will leave on Monday for Tours, France, and it is my hope that the coal proposition will soon again call him to London.

Lieutenant Colonel Chas. McKeehan, cousin of Miss Cora McKeehan of Chambersburg, PA, and cousin of Mrs. W. K. Sharpe, has been transferred to these headquarters to look after the claims, etc.

In peace times, Colonel McKeehan is a lawyer in Philadelphia, and also secretary of the Scotch-Irish Society. He is well known in Chambersburg, and Colonel Kennedy says between him and Colonel Byllesby, they think they can find enough to keep him busy.

On Sunday afternoon, November 3rd, I went to hear the concert in the Royal Albert Hall, and it is some hall.

Built between 1867–71, as a memorial of the prince consort at a cost of 200,000 pounds, it is one of the largest halls in the world and will comfortably seat eight thousand people, with another eleven hundred in the orchestra. Though frequently used for political demonstrations and other great gatherings, it is principally famous for musical performances on a large scale. Not every singer or speaker emerges successfully from the ordeal of facing that vast audience. In the arena alone, there is space for one thousand persons, while the amphitheater holds nearly fourteen hundred. Above are three rows of boxes, many of them private property. The magnificent organ, built by Willis, has nearly nine thousand pipes. Concerts and recitals are frequently given on Sunday afternoons and evenings.

Directly in the rear of the hall hangs a very large gilt crown. I stepped back after the concert and had a talk with the usher. "That," he says, "is where the king sits, or rather that is his private stall." They do not call them boxes over here but stalls.

Then on the other side hang three large white feathers. They resemble an ostrich feather. "That," he says, "is where the Prince of Wales sits." He claims the building will hold fifteen thousand. I cannot say for sure, but I am positive it will hold more than eight thousand persons. It is capable of holding as many as the Mormon Temple. At least it is the finest concert hall I have ever seen and is spotlessly clean. The seats are all highly upholstered with red covering not exactly plush but something near it. They are soft and comfortable.

The concert was simply grand. There was a great crowd there but I cannot say it was packed. I judge there were about four thousand people there. It takes up promptly on time and leaves out on time. The lady singers were very good.

The conductor certainly has a well-trained orchestra. The applause was many, but they did not repeat any numbers.

And when they played "God Save the King" you can just imagine how it sounded. Everybody stands and sings. There are about one hundred and fifty in the orchestra alone. I think they have every kind of instrument there.

At Albert Memorial in Kensington Gardens, in talking with the officer there, he says that the monument cost more than Queen Victoria's. While hers is marble, this one is made from both marble and granite. I am in no position to agree or disagree about the price of it either. It is certainly a fine piece of work. To carve the likeness of all those great men as they have around that large monument is some work, and it surely did cost a lot of money, but it seems that these people have some way of getting money not known [to] others.

On the upper part of this hall they have a promenade where they walk around between numbers, and if you go there alone you can possibly come away with company if you so desire. Another nice part of the hall is that the seats are so arranged that everyone has a good view of the performance.

On Monday, November 4th, the good news came through and between 4 p.m. and 5 p.m., Captain W. S. Franklin dropped the double bars from his erect shoulders and placed thereon the gold leaf and from here on we will salute him as Major W. S. Franklin. Everybody is glad of the promotion, as he surely deserved it. Many nights during the embarkation of soldiers, he was up all night and then rode all night getting back to London, ate breakfast, and went at once to the office as an accommodation to the embarkation port of Liverpool. It was a very hard trip and it was hoped by the office clerks that he would get lieutenant colonel. But, we never get all that is coming to us in this world, so the thing is to be satisfied with what you get.

At 2:45 p.m. this same date the Japanese prince went away after visiting the king. He went from Victoria Station. They had a large bright red carpet on the sidewalk that covered it all over. He came to the station in an auto. The king was with him. He left by special train of four coaches, the blinds were drawn, and I could not get close enough to see much of the inside of the coaches through the end windows.

He went to Folkstone, and from there to Paris. He had his entire suite of fourteen people and when they departed, the Japanese flag over the Rubens Hotel was at once withdrawn.

They have been drawing guns past this office building now for four days, so Tuesday, I thought I would hunt them up. I found that they were placing them on the Mall that is the street that runs from Admiralty Arch on the NE Corner of Hyde Park past St. James Palace to Buckingham Palace, and is about one mile long.

These guns have all been captured from the Germans, and they are stored in double file order the entire length and the other side single file about half way on the NE side of the Mall. They are still coming, and there will be about six hundred when they all get here. There are guns of all descriptions, large and small. They are pulled by the trucks, the same ones that we saw coming through our hometown, some months ago.

Some are broken at the barrel, some have the trigger taken off them, and whatever damage the Germans could do to them they did when they saw they were to be captured.

But, most of them are in very good condition and could easily be fixed up and used again.

Most of them are camouflaged, painted in broad black and white stripes. The saying here is that to airships those colors are very hard to see from the distance they fly. They all look and show that they have seen hard service.

The great rumor today is that the Germans have signed the armistice. The people are certainly tired of this war and they can hardly hold in. They feel like celebrating, but the old kaiser is so foxy that they are fearful of believing it.

The dope is that the American troops are five miles from the only opening that the Germans are making for, and the English are fifteen miles on their front from this same hole, and the French are in the front driving the Germans; and as one of the officers said in the office this afternoon, they are "between the devil and the deep blue sea." At any rate, the Germans cannot hold out much longer. Houser and Smith continue to bid me good-bye.

I am somewhat disappointed over not receiving any word as to the outcome of the election of the governorship of Pennsylvania. I can hardly think my dear friend Senator Sproul was defeated. I had thought we would get some cable on Wednesday, and this is Thursday. No word received yet.

But since writing, I hunted a Red Cross bulletin and it shows Senator Sproul elected. It gives no majority, and I care nothing about that, just so he gets in, and for once more the dear old state of Pennsylvania does what was right and put into that office a clean man. He should have a new chair though and not use the one that the former used. And I am also sure that he will not care for his eyebrows to grow quite so long as the other gentleman.

Now, it looks like the people are getting their eyes open and I trust they will look after the proper candidate for the president in 1920, cause I think that really Senator, I mean, Governor Sproul is just the man. He won't give all the banks and the railroads to his sons-in-law and make a regular family affair out of the White House. He is too clean a man for that.

I would have willingly went across the pond to work for his election had it been necessary. But, I did my part. I helped him put "Denny" out for the full count.

As soon as I saw that Red Cross bulletin, I said Mr. M. K. Burgner and Mr. W. O. Nicklas were surely on the job, as I am always sure they can deliver Franklin County in the column they want, and they always know who are the proper people.

Won't that be a happy meeting when Lieutenant Jack Sproul comes home from the front? When he tells his mother and father how he was gassed and how Colonel Kennedy wrote the news to his father for him. Maybe I didn't play ball while that was going on. I knew that was an important matter and I never let a telegram get cold. In fact, everybody played ball. The colonel just provided the information and everybody was on their toes.

And while I wished to be there to help this time, I would have willingly voted blind, lame, and possibly using the names of dead men if I could to see him win. But, it was turned over to Mr. M. K. Burgner and Mr. W. O. Nicklas, and they delivered the goods, and the country is once more saved.

CHAPTER 5

Victory Pageant in London: Greatest Lord Mayor's Show, November 9, 1918

Well, the people here have been talking about this day for a long time, and I have been somewhat anxious to just see what they call a big time.

As I understand it, the Lord Mayor is elected every year and on the ninth of November of each year they have this sort of parade. The last three years of this time they have had naval and military features, but they were nothing compared with what they had yesterday. The people knew the war was won and they cheered themselves hoarse as the emblems of victory passed them on the streets.

The procession was two miles long and they went from Guild Hall, which is in front of Westminster Abbey, to the Law Court which is through the Strand to Fleet Street. The sidewalks were lined with people the like I have never seen in my life. The Peace Jubilee in Philadelphia was considered a very large gathering, but truly that is only a drop in the bucket to the people in this place.

It is absolutely impossible to describe to anyone the mass of people here in London. It looks like they could have fought the war for four more years and have plenty left.

There are plenty of representatives from all the Dominions of Britain and there were about four thousand soldiers in line. The cheers that greeted the men and women in line showed the feelings the people had for them after this four-year war.

The parade route was changed a little to accommodate the masses of people. The Lord Mayor, Sir Horace Marshall, is the principal in the firm Marshall & Son, wholesale agents and publishers, on Temple Street. The parade passed his firm so that his employees might witness it and give him three cheers, which they certainly did.

In the morning, the colonel told me I should see the parade, to which of course, I filed no objections. I noticed in the paper the route of the parade, so I went down the embankment to Temple Street. The crowd was something awful.

The embankment is along the Thames River; I referred to it in other places. I think you can see what I mean. A large crowd went up Temple Street. I followed. Being well up in front, I was among the first there. The mob continued to gather and the pushing became so great several women began to faint. One very close to me began a spell of coughing. A soldier just out of the hospital began sneezing. Quite a bit of the parade had passed and as I had a good place, I hated to part with it. The lady began going down, which was hard to do as they were packed like sardines in a box. A man said to me to try to help to hold her. I thought now here, it is no place for Roy. She might be some man's wife near here. He might see me and start something, and the colonel is not here. I will have some time explaining. I quietly left the lady to the other men and I squeezed out from there. The flu is as great here as can be and I had no business getting sick, the colonel told me so I know he meant it. And, you know holding a white woman when they faint ain't no job for a colored man.

I ran around to another street (forgot the name of it—some square, it was) and finished seeing the parade from there.

After the representatives of the Navy and Marines came bands galore. The Royal Air Force, with a captured Albatross (German) and types of British planes and airships. On motor lorries were samples of air bombs with which Londoners are very familiar.

All during the parade there was a fleet of aeroplanes flying at a high altitude over the city. There were thirteen in the fleet and four large observation balloons near the river. Two torpedo boats were lying in the river, and two large balloons passed over St. Paul's Cathedral.

The applause was especially strong for the Red Cross ladies. There was a float showing the work of the ladies in the munition plants and another float where women were making aeroplane wings during the parade. The main thing that attracted the attention was a long string of captured German guns. All the guns bore battle scars and were camouflaged in the curious manner adopted in the war. Some were green and yellow, black and white, and many other colors.

Another feature of the parade was a pigeon loft. The public has been allowed to know a little of the great work done by these feathered soldiers of war, and they were given a hearty cheer.

Of course, the parade did look very good and I told many of the people that I talked to that it was fine. That is what they expect you to say, and [I] did not want to disappoint them. I have no thought of them reading this book of mine, but truly I was much disappointed in myself on what these people call a wonderful parade. I was really afraid to say so at first, being such a small fish. I listened carefully until I heard several of the important people speak, and then I knew my judgment of the affair was right. It was a regular big show parade and very little was shown of what America has done in this war.

Just before writing this, I went over to the Mall and walked from Queen Victoria's monument to the Arch at Trafalgar Square and looked at the guns there, to see if there were any marked that the American soldiers had taken. Find nothing doing. I then walked up to the Mall to Hyde Park corner and nothing doing. There are now about six hundred and some guns there, and nine inside the yard at Buckingham Palace. They are of all sizes and descriptions and many of them are marked by who or rather what company they were taken by. Everything shines but America. Two hundred and ten millimeter is the largest there now. They are still bringing them in.

Well, the mob that is looking at the guns today is wonderful, and if you want to know anything about them just ask the kids. They are there galore, working every part they can move. I don't think any mother has any troubles with her boys today, for I think they are all around the guns.

CHAPTER 6

THE DOWNFALL
OF KAISER BILL

For about two months it has been known around here that the old fellow was very shaky and could hardly hold out much longer than Christmas. This wonderful Transportation Department continued to bring the troops in by the thousands.

No play after the United States made up their minds to go into this fight. They came over here to play the game and they have done it, although you won't hear that said very loud on this side.

We came over here to work and fight twenty-six hours every day, and not to start to fight at 9:00 a.m. and stop for Tea at 4:00 p.m., and the results show for themselves.

General Allenby went into the Holy Lands at Palestine and made things too hot for them there. Then Turkey went into the air, Austria flew the coop, and the colonel told me one morning we will get after that other Turkey shortly. On Friday, November 8th, he hollered "Kamerad," and General Pershing said "We, We." It is all over but the shouting, which will happen this week.

And every morning at the mess at 14 Great Cumberland Place, there was a talk as to how long it would be before it would come. The officers there always differed, but the colonel said, "Home by Xmas." The clerks have been telling me good-bye for three weeks now, but just how long it will take to fix the papers secure cannot yet be said.

So far as the English papers are concerned, there is nothing to it but Foch. But, I think to myself, which I have a right to, that the head of the

American Army in England should have a say, as he sure can draw up some papers that will hold you tight.

About two weeks ago, everything was slated by Germany for a large sea fight and the fleet was ordered out but instead they mutinied and refused to come, and the arm that was going to try the last gambling stroke became paralyzed and they put up the Red Flag. Today, half the German fleet have up the Red Flag and nearly all their forts.

And now that the whole matter is settled, we will see what the countries involved think of America.

My chances for getting to Berlin do not look so bright just now, but the shouting next week might bring on something not yet seen.

CHAPTER 7

THE SHOUTING

The Armistice was handed to Germany to sign late Friday evening November 8th, and [the kaiser] was given seventy-two hours to sign it.

Of course, it was known here that there was nothing else to it but for him to sign. His entire army was just about in the hands of the American troops, and escape was impossible. So on Monday morning at 5:00 a.m. the old fellow, the kaiser, came across and signed. Colonel Kennedy was officially notified by the British War Office shortly after his arrival at his office that the papers were properly signed. In turn, he notified Major Franklin, and in about one hour the bells began to ring. Clerks deserted the offices, particularly the women, and the celebrating began. Flags were everywhere. They had been put away, as the English had just about given up hope of needing them. Some of the girl messengers in the building began crying, as they did not understand what the bells meant.

In a short time, the streets were jam packed with people. I slipped to Buckingham Palace. The king and queen were in the yard. A large crowd was in front of the palace. The king and queen stood and waved a white handkerchief to the throng. Guards were doubled around the yard. They also shook hands with a few that had called to pay their respects, and were admitted to the yard.

The royal band came out, and walking past the palace played "Smile, Smile, Smile." Everybody was singing the same thing. Soldiers were dancing on the streets with the girls.

Every taxi, wagon, auto, anything that could move carried a load of women and men on the tops, on the fenders, backs, and the seats were simply crowded.

About two hundred American soldiers holding a large American flag marched past the office building singing, "Hail, Hail, the Gang's all here . . ." You know the rest, and they didn't care, either.

The Strand was a solid mass of people. A phone message from Paris says it is the same thing over there.

And now, down in front of the office building, the crowd is terrible. It has begun to rain and has gotten very foggy. A motorcar with sidecar that should hold two persons holds six now.

Monday, November 11th, 1918, the prime minister made the following announcement:

The Armistice was signed at five o'clock this morning and Hostilities are to cease on all fronts at 11:00 a.m. today.

LLOYD GEORGE.

Along about the first part of October, while things were going the right way, when the Transportation question was at its greatest and just when they needed the right stripe of men to deliver the goods, a change was made that was certainly interesting to me.

Captain M. C. Kennedy was made Terminal Superintendent at Brest, France. I had been thinking of France, since I had seen most of London, and now I wanted there. Well, the passport part kept me from getting out of this country, and both Chief Clerk Houser and Sergeant Smith have suggested to me to go over in one of the aeroplanes that go over from here frequently, but that does not sound exactly clear to me. I am willing to go when the proper time comes, but I really do not want to take that chance now.

But I am wild to see Brest, and it looks now that the colonel is just as interested, so much that he might cross over to look at the place. So, I am sleeping happy over the thought that I am going to see France before I return to the states.

I had thought I would wait a while before writing this up, as I feel that he will shortly have the title of major. In my way of thinking, he should get promoted. There is no question about him making good. He just simply cannot help it. Being a chip off the old block, it comes natural to him.

While all this good news is coming in, along comes the pleasant news that Lieutenant T. B. Kennedy Jr., has been made a captain. He is

Members of a Services of Supply (SOS) regiment take a break from their work detail to pose for a photographer. More than 150,000 African American members of the SOS regiments were stationed in port towns on the coast of France. In Brest, St. Nazaire, and Bordeaux, these regiments were responsible for ditch digging, repairing roads and bridges, and collecting the dead. Author's collection stationed at St. Dizier, France. Between Brest and St. Dizier, these stations have seen the hardest part of the transportation problem. Each was under hard and trying circumstances. It shows he made good.

And right behind that comes a letter to the colonel from one of his friends in France, Colonel J. A. McCrea, saying that if the colonel sent me over to him, he would use me on his private car, which he will have out shortly. It is the only private car in France. Now you can well imagine what I am thinking of. I am simply clear up a tree. The act of being on a private car certainly appeals to me, but I don't like the thoughts of being in France unless the colonel is going to be there, too. Unless, it is to be only for a short time.

He told me to think it over. I am trying to do that but it is one hard nut for me to crack. It is no easy task to go to a different gentleman after working so long and learning the disposition of one family and friends. It is easy to think of the nice parts, but the other parts have to be reckoned with as well.

What will come out of the private car matter remains to be seen. I cannot say or decide it right now.

We have now had three days of celebrating since the news came of the signing of the Armistice. Three days of joy. Tuesday night they had a large bonfire at Trafalgar Square. Everything that would burn, and that they could get their hands on, was put on the fire. The brushes that the street cleaners were using were taken from them and thrown on the fire.

Trafalgar Square was also covered with beautiful flowers. One of the buses broke down and was pushed into the fire. People that were in it were lucky enough to get out in time. While the feeling was running at the highest, Major Franklin very politely fired the cook at the mess. And now, with the assistance of the maid, I will try to get their stomachs back into the proper condition again.

These people are doing the best they know how to with their celebrating, but it is plain they do not know like America does. They are unable to get a band here, as the men of music ability are nearly all at the front, except the king's regular band, and of course, they cannot use that.

Mobs gather in front of Buckingham Palace every day. I saw the king and queen, and Princess Mary when they went out to drive in their auto. They waved to the people, who waved in return.

This is Wednesday night, and all day they have still been bringing in guns. This has been going on all week.

Sunday, November 17th. Well, this has been one of those weeks in London. Things have certainly been going on. I saw the king on Monday, Tuesday afternoon, Wednesday, and Friday, and only missed him by a close margin on Saturday. I would like to go to St. Paul's tonight where he will be there for services, but I have to wait dinner at the mess this evening. After dinner, it will be too late; but I do not mind that at all. It would be pretty rich for Roy to be at the same services with the king and queen.

Well, the celebrants are just commencing to cool down. The police had to call the soldiers in to help them. The crowds commenced to get rough and break windows on the trams, and other damages. They had their final dance in Hyde Park last night, and they sang every song that I think they knew, and dances that never have been seen in the States were done last night.

On Thursday there were two barrels of real apples arrived from the garden spot of the world. And at once my job started to increase. Colonel Kennedy and Major Franklin made out a list of those to be remembered. I was sent to buy baskets that would hold a nice number of apples. I got them and took them to the mess, then I got the list, and an auto was gotten for me because you never could walk to all the places. Next, you would be mobbed and the apples taken from you. So with a driver, I started.

I think in going to the different places, I covered nearly the whole city. The apples were very well received at every place. You might know they were when I saw that apples like that cost two shillings apiece. You might think that is strong, but it is not. No apple can be gotten like what we received for less than two shillings and in the first-class stores they will cost 2–6. In American money that is about sixty-two cents.

At all the places the people went wild over the apples and the phone was kept busy in the afternoon thanking the colonel and major for the apples. They were certainly beauties. Well, that they were from the Cumberland Valley is sufficient alone to know they were the best. Out of the two barrels, they packed were so well that there were only nine bruised apples. However, they were not bruised too badly for Roy to eat.

When the apples were delivered to the mess, colonel told me to knock the head in. I did so and looked and just thought, "Oh you beauties from home." At once I thought of the officers of that Eagle Mountain Orchard Company. I fixed up the baskets as ordered until I came to the Grimes Golden apples. Then I called the colonel on the phone and told him I had the red apples all out of the first barrel, down to the Grimes Golden apples, or rather they looked like Grimes. I also said I do not think they will keep so long, as there are indications that they won't. He said, "How do they taste?" Well, I said, "I have not tasted them yet, but they look all right."

I thought he might ask me that so I played safe and did not taste them until after. He then told me to keep them for him and only pack the red ones to take out. Of course he knew that Roy was going to eat an apple and he did not mind that; so after I was through and satisfied the job was right, or rather one hundred percent, I got very busy on a real apple.

After every bite of the apple, I looked at it and said Messrs. C. M. Davison, F. W. Hankins, and F. B. Reed, owners of the Eagle Mountain Orchard Company, "these CV men are the real cheese." When I brought one basketful to the office building, the women on the car wanted to take them from me, and I knew if I met a bunch of soldiers, it would be all up with me.

When I went to Sir Albert and Lady Stanley, on South Street near Hyde Park (I always made sure I was at the right place) she came to the door. As I handed them in with a card she says, "Well, and you are from Virginia?" I said, "No, Miss, from Pennsylvania." She said, "Well, I have not seen a little black boy for so long." She said, "Wait a minute." She went into the house and returned—of course you know I waited all right—out she came with a Half Crown and said, "Take this. I am certainly glad to see a little black boy."

I thanked her very politely and thought, "Lady Stanley, if you want to hand me Sir Albert Stanley's money, you can look at this black boy as long as you want," cause money sure does slip through your fingers here in this place.

This Sir and Lady business I did not understand, so I asked Mr. Houser where did it come from. He said the king bestows that on people. Well, I knew he bestowed the V.C. and D.O.S. and such things of a military nature, but I did not know about the other.

Sir Albert Stanley is one of the large men of this country and had formerly been from the States, where he was connected with the trolley business and also railway in Detroit, Mich.

He is now president of the Board of Trade and a member of Parliament and other things. But one thing I do know. He is short that 2–6 that Lady Stanley handed over to me.

When I went to "The Albany" on Piccadilly, with a packet to Captain Wilmot, I think that was the name, anyhow, I got the right man. He thanked me very kindly and spoke so pleasantly of colonel. His clerks also spoke so nicely of him. On my way to the elevator, a rather elderly lady stopped me and said, "Excuse me but are you from the States?" I said, "Yes." Of course, I had off my hat as soon as she spoke. She said, "And you are delivering apples from there?" I said, "Yes, ma'am." She said, "It's so singular, I do the same thing. My daughter, Mrs. Henderson, lives in the Catskill Mountains in New York and she sends me two barrels every year in December; and I take them to my friends here in London." She asked me who is my boss and right here the history of Colonel M. C. Kennedy went right out and believe me, I did not need any book. When I was through she said "Oh, how intelligent you are!" Can you beat that? Well I just thought that was the first time I ever heard that and never thought anyone would think that. When it comes to explaining some of these things I have seen here in London, I only see how short I am.

Well, I was about four hours delivering the apples. I only missed the king by a few minutes as he was going to the Royal Albert Hall to services with the queen and Princess Mary. I was coming from Regent Park from Mr. Coe's to the Royal Albert Mansions.

Today I took a box of apples to Mr. Charles Palmer at Lewisham, which is a suburb of London. I went out on the train from Charing Cross Station, but came back in a tram. It is about twenty-five miles and it looks more like a hometown than anything I have seen since I came over. Everybody has a front yard and some of them have gardens and some grass. The houses are small. I found the place I was looking for and as I went in, a longhaired dog gave the signal with his mouth, and up comes an ugly, big shepherd dog showing me his teeth. I talked dog talk to him right strong for a while, hoping someone from the house would come and finish. But nothing doing. I finally out-talked him and he walked away and I went on to the door and was admitted.

The maids came into the room and began a long talk with me. One thing, over here everybody is anxious to hear of the US, and they are of the thought that everybody over here is wealthy. They feel surprised when you tell them different. Well, I talked to them for about a half hour, and then Mr. Palmer came down. I don't know whether he has any title or not, but he talked very smoothly and kindly, and very agreeably deposited five shillings in my hand and said, "Get a drink on your way to town." He would get a title very quick if it was left to me.

He said he would see the colonel tomorrow and he thanked me very kindly for bringing the apples to him. I over-thanked him both going and coming.

Also today the colonel told me to bring two baskets of apples down to the office for Mr. Houser to take to Honorable Sir F. W. Hankins's relatives. They went to see them this afternoon. I hope they got there all right with them. They also want to take this book to them to read, as they have told them I am writing it. If there is anything they lose, I want it to not be the book, anyhow.

Sergeant Warren E. Smith, the Master Engineer in the office here, was with President Flagler of the Florida East Coast Railway. Well, he went blind before he died, and the one that succeeded him also went blind, so Smith often speaks of that as hard luck, but I told him, "Oh, brother don't you worry. This one we have here never will go blind. Not this colonel. He has some eyes. He can see clean through a well and see if you are busy—don't worry about that."

Some few weeks ago, Lieutenant Colonel Wentz was here and the colonel gave a dinner in honor of him. I was waiting the table and I was as happy as a lark. About the middle of the dinner I noticed I had lost one of the pearl buttons out of the sleeve of my white coat. I had thought, Oh well, I will use my right hand mostly to wait, anyhow, and the boss won't see it. Mrs. Kennedy's eyes are about as sharp as his but I sort of think he has a shade the best vision on me anyhow. Well, I was going right through and after dinner he and Major Franklin called me in the rear parlor. My heart began to flutter but they said, "Roy, you handled the dinner fine." "Got through very nicely," said the colonel. Well then, that was it, I thought. I will get another button when I go to my room tonight and in the morning I will be all right.

Well, I did so. In the morning while I was putting on his puttees and lacing up his shoes, he was reading his papers. All at once he held the paper away and said, "Roy, what became of the button off your coat sleeve last night? Haven't you got any?" Well it hit me like thunder hit the toad. I could not look up. If there had been a hole in the floor, I would have went right through.

I could not laugh, and I could hardly keep from it. You see, what I was thinking was Mrs. Kennedy was not there, and I could pass him all right. I could hardly find the hole to lace the shoe from laughing. Of course, this all happened in a second. I finally got it out that I had lost it and had gotten another one.

He went on reading the paper. Now, let me tell you nothing passes that eye.

On Wednesday, November 20th, Major Franklin went to Liverpool to superintend the embarkation of soldiers for the States. He says that he never saw such a wild bunch of men so anxious to get home. The officers say the men ran five miles in about one hour and a quarter. They could not hold them back and they feared the boat would be loaded before they got there. We have sent about 4,400 out so far this week.

That wonderful ship *Minnekahda* was the first ship to take back to America soldiers from here after the war—and she is some boat, I mean.

Every person has a right to think, as long as you don't think too loud. As the home feeling is creeping up stronger in some very prominent people here. I see the *Leviathan* formerly the *Vaderland*, which was taken from Germany, is to sail from Liverpool this week for New York, and return and sail from Brest, France. Now, I have not heard anything, but I do know she is a fast boat and that she can go to New York in six or seven days. That home feeling has for the last four years called for special movements, fast runs, and as Captain J. C. Kennedy is at Brest, I am looking for the major emblems to fall to him shortly. I just have a little request that someone very important to me might make up their mind to go to Brest and sail on that ship.

I am satisfied that he will not be here a moment longer and can be relieved, as the most important work is now done. I hardly think it will be long here anymore.

I was very much surprised to have a long distance call on the phone a few days ago and hear that it was Captain J. C. Kennedy at Paris. He wanted to talk to his father. The line was very good and his voice was very familiar.

On Saturday, the king viewed about 20,000 silver badge men in Hyde Park. As I had a trip for downtown, I passed at the proper time and witnessed the affair.

When the king and queen are going to take a drive, you may as well give these people a holiday, cause they just gather and wait to salute him all over the route he is to take. They are surely loyal to their king.

On Thursday, November 28th, it was Thanksgiving: a day I thought was celebrated all over the World. I find it is not observed here—only by the American Forces. They had two hundred turkeys at the Eagle Hut and dinner was 2–6. They started to serve at 11:00 a.m., and at 7:30 p.m. the turkey had flown away. Then they served cold ham. The dinner was very nicely gotten up and the soldiers surely laid right to it.

Besides the show there was a dance after 9:30 p.m. by the Ladies Jazz Band. The American Red Cross provided dinner for all the American soldiers in the Great Britain Hospitals, with turkey and pumpkin pie. The turkeys all came from America on the Steamship *Leviathan*.

Services were held at St. Martin-in-the-Fields by the American and some British Forces. Ushers were supplied from all the different departments. Captain H. W. Atkinson, Personnel Officer of the Transportation Department, represented this branch at the services.

It was utterly impossible for Colonel Kennedy to be present at the services. He was too busy. Major Franklin wanted to be present but had to see to the loading of several ships that will sail very shortly. Major Neilson who has joined the T.C. was formerly of the PRR and is a shining light in his work, being one of those wide-awake transportation men. He wanted to go but had to look after some coaling of ships at the Royal Albert Dock. Captain Miller of the Merchants and Miners Transportation Company, he was one of the real shipping men, he just could not be spared in no way. He, with Major Franklin, can tell you how many soldiers a vessel can take care of. Lieutenant Mackenson threw up his hands and said he was over-run with work, so it all passed up to Captain H. W. Atkinson, who they all claimed was full of grace and the people person to represent this department. I am positive they were all sorry they could not be present. They looked it.

The joke today is that the captain does not remember the text the minister spoke on, or where it is found.

For some time I have been wanting to have chicken and waffles for the officers at the Mess. To be ready when the signal was given me, I wrote to Mrs. M. C. Kennedy's cook Mrs. Nannie Echenrode for the recipe for the waffles as she makes them for the family. I also asked for her recipe for Russian Salad Dressing. She promptly sent it over. Then I had all kinds of trouble in getting a waffle iron. I went to all the large stores and found none. Captain Frank Coville told me of several places, but they had none. Finally, I got in with the Chef at the US Navy Canteen, then my troubles ended. He told me I could [have] anything I wanted, and I got a waffle iron.

Sunday, November 24th, was the day the colonel told me I could have the feast. Well, I went after it right. I had three chickens and a large bowl of batter made up; you know women know how many they will have for a meal, but men never.

That chicken was cooked to the minute and the waffles were just right. I never spared the butter or lard in greasing the iron or baking powder in making up the batter. Well, the men said it was right and they know. The supper was for five—all officers. Lieutenant Commander Higgins had just received word that he would be relieved, and I think every officer that came in gave him some message to take back to the States for them. Must have smelled what was coming off.

At any rate, there were nine army and navy officers, who had eaten dinner before I was through. Which means, Roy was stepping some. When it was over, I went up to the sitting room and they told me it was the best meal they had since they left the States. They gave me cigars and cigarettes. Naval Constructor McBride ate sixteen waffles and that Major Franklin went ahead of him. He was sure of it. Lieutenant Commander Higgins says he stopped counting when he reached fourteen, but he was sure he would not need anything more to eat for about three days.

The other officers said they were glad to happen in at that time, and they hoped I would let them know the next time I cooked so they would try to have an excuse to visit the colonel.

There is one thing about these English homes that would sure set American women wild. That is the odor of cooking. It matters not what you cook, or how you try, the odor goes all through the house and out on the street. It is a common thing to pass a house and be able to tell what they are having for their meal. The kitchens are all in the basement. And why it goes through the house, I don't know but it does.

I also served scalloped potatoes and one of those real large homemade apple pies. They looked at the pie and said "Hold that for the next time. We can't go at it today."

The clerks in the office asked me to bring them a waffle. I promised but none was left.

Ice is used very little over here. When they are having dinners, and ice is needed for the appetizer, the colonel told me he did not mind me getting a piece of ice from the fish man. But, he did not care for me to get ice from the undertaker. He would not feel right in drinking anything off ice the undertaker used.

Major Franklin smoked his pipe. When he does that, he is pretty well interested.

On Friday evening, November 29th, Major W. S. Franklin gave a farewell dinner in honor of the departure of Lieutenant Commander John S. Higgins, who will leave here at 4:30 Saturday afternoon for Paris, then go to Brest, France, where he will sail on the "Big Boy" *Leviathan*, for the States about next Thursday, December 5th. This will be the first link broken in the quartette at 14 Great Cumberland Place and you know everyone was sorry to see him go. He has been here for a long time and you know the most popular occupation in these days is the paymaster. This makes him more popular. The whole house had to listen to the wonderful things that that little boy of his would do when he saw daddy. It was some fun.

Those present: Colonel M. C. Kennedy, Major Franklin, Major E. S. Neilson, Captain L. G. Miller, Captain H. W. Atkinson, Captain Strong, Lieutenant G. R. Williams, Lieutenant C. T. Mackenson, Lieutenant Commander John S. Higgins.

Naval Constructor McBride had expected to be present but Admiral Sims is pretty sick and that holds Commander McBride some closer; but one thing about the Navy, they understand each other and they sure have some organization, the best ever.

This represents the main strength of the transportation department that handled the soldiers on this side and that made the kaiser throw up his hands.

I have told you of Major Franklin, and the colonel you all know. Major Neilson came from the PRR and you know nothing but the best come from the PRR. He has the handling of the docks in the best of conditions. They are simply perfect.

Major Miller comes from the Merchants and Miners Transportation Company and we know that is some company. He has handled all their large vessels and been stationed in Baltimore, Philadelphia, New York, and Boston. He has experience plenty.

Lieutenant Williams—well, he hails from Georgia and Florida, and when he gets that large cigar and starts to dictate that stenog's pen has got to go some—and he is certainly some hustler and I must also say the brand he smokes is there in quality, as he often says "Roy, have a smoke." And I have been too well raised to refuse.

Now as to Lieutenant Mackenson, well you know he was raised in the Cumberland Valley and made by the Cumberland Valley Railroad Company, so he is one hundred and twenty-five percent. Now, is there any wonder how or when the colonel wanted any information, how he could get it?

Well, it was some dinner. Turkey and all that went with it and trimmings of various kinds and brands.

When I helped Commander Higgins down with his trunk, he said that he had not thought of it or he would have had Colonel Kennedy and Major Franklin carry his trunks down instead of taking exercise in the morning.

The colonel told Lieutenant Higgins that he was the first to pack up and that he should be moderate in what he took, so as to give someone else a chance at bringing a few things.

Captain Atkinson in peacetime is with the B & ORR and of course the B & O has some good men, too. His experience just fits in here, as the personnel officer. He is a real hustler and is full of pep.

Well, today, Sunday, December 1st, M. Clemenceau and Marshall Foch arrived in London, and the welcome they received will certainly last them in memory for years. The houses along the route of parade were all decorated with flags and bunting, and the people simply yelled themselves hoarse. They waved handkerchiefs and hats as the parade passed. They rode in carriages drawn by beautiful bay horses. The entire route of the parade was lined with soldiers that kept the crowd back, and when it comes to handling large crowds of people these people are there with the goods. The different guards are well drilled and know just what to do.

Well, as my time of being in London is getting short, we will likely, as the colonel says, "receive some marching orders soon."

On Friday, December 6th, Colonel M. C. Kennedy and Major W. S. Franklin and Roy left Charing Cross Station at 11:05 a.m. for Paris, France, arriving at Folkestone at 1:10 p.m. I got through the custom officials without very much trouble, as my passports were all right, and a few words to the proper people by Major Franklin helped to straighten things out.

We took the boat *Vindicto* across the Channel, which was real smooth. It is somewhat dangerous now in crossing at these times, on account of floating mines. They have one or two gunners who ride the boats and keep a lookout, and they shoot them with a rifle, which makes them explode. We were fortunate enough not to have any trouble with any. The boats I find run very fast, making about twenty-five knots per hour. And on water you will find that is going at a pretty good pace. It is about thirty-one miles across the channel at this point. We docked at Boulogne, France, at about 4:45 p.m. It is a very nice harbor. The boats all turn around and back in. There were quite a good many soldiers on the boat, and in talking to some I find they are going to Cologne, Germany, to help

FORM No. 176b—CONSULAR.
(Corrected June, 1917.)

Fee for Passport.....................$1.00
Fee for administering oath and preparing passport application... 1.00

EMERGENCY PASSPORT APPLICATION.

NATIVE.

No. 10164   Issued ....December.4,.1918............
                                                          (Date)

I, Royal..Augustus..Chapman............, a NATIVE AND LOYAL CITIZEN OF THE UNITED STATES, hereby apply to the American ....Embassy........., at ....London............, for an emergency passport for myself, accompanied by my wife,—...................................., and minor children, as follows :............................., born at ...., on the .... day of ....;
                                                                          (Month and year.)
and ...., born at ...., on the .... day of .... ;
                                                                          (Month and year.)
and ....

I solemnly swear that I was born at..Chambersburg......, in the State of ....Pennsylvania.... on April.4,.1875.........,* that my {father}{husband} ....Royal.Christian................, was born in .....Lynchburg,..Virginia. and is now residing at..Chambersburg,.Penn...., for the purpose of..Laborer............;† [that he emigrated to the United States from the port of ...., on or about ....; that he resided .... years
                                                          (Date.)
uninterruptedly, in the United States, from .... to ...., at ....; that
                                        (Year.) (Year.)
he was naturalized as a citizen of the United States before the ...., Court of ...., at ...., on ....,
                                                                  (Date.)
as shown by the Certificate of Naturalization presented herewith];‡ that I am the bearer of Passport No.———, issued by ....——————...................... on ....;
that my legal domicile is in....Chambersburg,.Pennsylvania, my permanent residence being at ....Chambersburg,.Pennsylvania. I last left the United States on .July.18,.1918.....,
                                                                          (Date)
arriving at ...England............, ..., on ..August.3,.1918. where I am now
                (Town, province.)   (Country.)   (Date)
residing for the purpose of.Personal.servant...., on behalf of ....
Colonel M.C.Kennedy, Deputy Director General of Transportation firm,
American.forces.in.England..
(corporation, or other organization represented, if any.)
that I have resided outside the United States at the following places for the following periods :§
...England....................., from .....July.1918...to.date.....
...., from ....to..........................;
...., from ....to..........................;
and that I desire to remain a citizen of the United States and intend to return thereto permanently to reside and perform the duties of citizenship within four {months}{years} or when...................

I have not applied elsewhere for a United States passport or for consular registration and been refused.
I desire a passport for use in visiting the countries hereinafter named for the following purpose :

United Kingdom   Accompanying Colonel M.C.Kennedy
(Name of country.)   (Object of visit.)

France
(Name of country.)   (Object of visit.)

....
(Name of country.)   (Object of visit.)

OATH OF ALLEGIANCE.

Further, I do solemnly swear that I will support and defend the Constitution of the United States against all enemies, foreign and domestic; that I will bear true faith and allegiance to the same; and that I take this obligation freely, without any mental reservation or purpose of evasion: So help me God.

                              Royal A. Christian
                              (Signature of applicant.)

American ....Embassy............at ....London...............

Sworn to before me this ....4th.... day of....December.1918....
                                              (Month and year.)

                              W.M......................
                              (Name.)

[SEAL.]   ....
                              (Title.)

*A person born in the United States should submit a birth certificate with his application, or, if the birth was not officially recorded, affidavits from the attending physician, parents, or other persons having actual knowledge of the birth.
†If the applicant's father was born in this country, lines should be drawn through the blanks in brackets.
‡It is desirable, but not absolutely necessary, that the certificate of naturalization of the father be submitted.
§See circular instruction of July 26, 1910, entitled "Protection of Native Americans Residing Abroad."

1—81

DESCRIPTION OF APPLICANT.

Age: 43 years.

Stature: 5 feet, 5 inches. Eng.

Forehead: Medium

Eyes: Black

Nose: Broad

Mouth: Full

Chin: Square

Hair: Black

Complexion: Colored

Face: Oval

Slight Scar on right cheek.

IDENTIFICATION.

December 4, 1918.
(Date.)

I, M. C. Kennedy, solemnly swear that I am a { native / naturalized } citizen of the United States; that I reside at US Army; that I have known the above-named Royal A. Christian personally for 15 years and know { him / her } to be a native citizen of the United States; and that the facts stated in { his / her } affidavit are true to the best of my knowledge and belief.

M. C. Kennedy

Colonel, Deputy Director
(Address of Witness)

American Embassy at London

Sworn to before me this 4th day of December, 1918.
(Month and year.)

[SEAL.]

Wm. Hammer
(Name.)

(Title.)

Identifying documents submitted as follows: *

Seaman's certificate of American citizenship. No. 1504 July 19, 1918.
Collector of Customs, New York.
Seaman's Identification Card 34832 July 19, 1918.
Military Registration Certificate.
References: Wilson Bell, 557 South Main Street, Chambersburg, Penn.
* See General Instruction No. 483, circular September 28, 1916, section 4.
David Robinson, 424 East Washington St. Chambersburg, Penn.

Letter from Col. M. C. Kennedy on file. to the effect that this colored man has been his servant for fifteen years, vouching for him in every way, and showing necessity of his accompanying him as his person servant in France.

A duplicate of the photograph to be attached hereto should be filed with the application retained in the office by which the emergency passport is issued.

One phot...
in this spac...
who takes...
must be in...
to cover on...

Royal Augustus Christian (whose name was mistyped as Chapman) filed this emergency passport application on December 4, 1918, so he could take up his duties as aide to Colonel M. C. Kennedy in France. It provides important information about his father and his occupation in England, and also attests to his good character in fifteen years' civilian service to Kennedy.
Division of Passport Control: Emergency Passport Applications, 1906–1925, Entry A1 544, General Records of the Department of State, Record Group 59. Courtesy of National Archives and Records Administration, College Park, Maryland

maintain order there. They, of course, were sore at being ordered there. Can you blame them?

Major Franklin told me to get up to the first part of the deck, so as to be one of the first in seeing the French official who comes aboard and examines all passports. As there are a great many people passing or traveling now, it takes some time to look them over. I went as ordered, and found out there was, I guess, about one hundred in line. I was about the tenth when I saw a soldier coming looking straight at me and said, "You are Roy?" I said, "Yes." He said, "Give me your passports and you go with your colonel and major." I handed them over and said to myself, the wires are being worked some place. I went to them and very shortly the soldier came back with all papers and handed them over, and loads of time was saved.

Well, I just as well tell you here as any place else, I have been with the colonel for a long time and have been around many of his friends, and they are many. But, let me say that Major W. S. Franklin is one of the brightest I ever saw. He is entitled to the A class. I have taken particular notice of him many times and just sort of studied him. Well, when he is done pulling wires, there is little left.

The colonel and the major went to the hotel for dinner. I went up the streets and looked the town over for a short while. You go across a long bridge and the streets are very narrow. After walking for quite some distance, I asked a policeman a few questions, but just about then this "jabbering" in French came up. Up to this time, had been talking with British and American soldiers.

I looked at this French soldier or policeman and the way he was reciting "Shakespeare" and going through the acts was wonderful. He was pointing to this and that. I looked and looked. I forgot all the French I studied back in the states, and sounds are all different than anything I ever heard. I finally said "All right" and shook my head to say all right, too, and offered him a cigarette, which he accepted, and I left that part of town.

I came over to the station and began to talk to the American soldiers that are on duty there, and I heard all kinds of things that had taken place with the American forces, of their being taken from place to place in the box cars, and their eating "Corn Wooley" and hard tacks. At about 8:30 p.m. about seventy-five Frenchmen who had been prisoners of war were released and were on their way home. They were at the station. They were glad to see the American soldiers and they told them some awful tales of their suffering. One soldier could speak enough French to get the story. He told the other soldiers and myself what was being said. They have certainly been handled very badly.

The train for Paris was due to leave Boulogne at 10:17 p.m. and the party came about 9:15 p.m. and shortly after that we all go through the gates for the train.

As it took some little time for the people to unload, particularly from the sleeping cars, I was unable to get into the train before it was packed like sardines in a box. America never would allow such packing of trains as they do over here. There were many soldiers on the train. The aisles were all filled with men, women, and children, all standing. The seats on the trains here all run crossways. They are supposed to hold five persons on each side. Well, they had the five on and there were four or five standing in the center. A military policeman was with me trying to find me a seat, and it was simply impossible to get a seat. An admiral and captain of the US Navy were also there without reservations, and he could not find a seat. So, I reported that to Major Franklin and he told me to come in the next section. Now that he and the colonel were all fixed, I was perfectly satisfied and contented.

There was a soldier there that, when he saw me talking to the major, he pitched in and told the major he would bring me with him. He also tried to get on the train but could not make it. The major told him all right, and I was looking to see how many were left. There were about fifty people in all. The second section followed in about fifteen minutes and I got on with the Naval officers and this little soldier who knew everybody of any consequence, who was making it for New York City. Well, he was all mouth.

The train pulled out, everything was all right, and it ran for about forty miles before she made a stop. Then a great mob of Belgian people, who had left their homes, got on with large bundles of clothing tied up in sheets and quilts. Mostly women, some trying to cry, others crying. Then a few stations further a number of men got on. And they came into the section I was in. As they talked, you could get a word here and there. The conversation was mostly of their troubles and of their homes destroyed.

As the train goes through Amiens, I was anxious to see what could be seen, but it was too dark. Nothing was to be seen at any of the towns we passed through that night, and in the morning we were through the bombed section.

I arrived at Paris at 8:15 p.m. After looking over the station, I got a taxi and went at once to the Hotel Meurice and asked for the party. The word came back telling me to come up to the room, which I of course expected. I went up and there I see Captain T. B. Kennedy Jr. He was looking fine and every inch a soldier.

The colonel and the major asked me how long I had been in the city. As they had just gotten in the hotel, they thought possibly I got in ahead of them, but they were just about fifteen minutes ahead of me.

Captain T. B. K. then asked me how I got through and how I liked this part of the country. He told me that Captain J. C. Kennedy had sailed for home. I was sorry to hear that in a way, as I sort of think I was slated to see Brest, France, on this trip. But it will not be long now I feel. At any rate, he will be glad to get home.

Captain T. B. K. has a long job yet and will likely not get away for some time. An average of 100,000 men per month have passed through his station for the last three months. Sure that takes head work to keep things well oiled that no one falls down. He looks well and seems to be quicker and seems to grasp the thought faster.

He tells the officers when he wants anything from the French, he goes after them. And, if they take things all right, everything comes across all right. But, if they fly up in the air, he just says he does not understand them, and lets them cool down. But, in the end he always finds them doing just what he wanted done, or what he asked them to do.

He had some time trying to bluff the flu, so he went to bed for two days and he and the flu fought it out. He won out, and the flu left him. He is still stationed at St. Dizier. They call it Dizzy, and the freight comes marked Dizzy.

He asked me how much French I knew. I told him my French was limited, as it seemed my pronunciations were all wrong. One day one of the German aeroplanes was flying over the station near him and lost a flyers suit. He later got it and expected to use it, but it was called for later, and his expectations in that respect were lost.

First Lieutenant Alex Stevenson, of the Royal Air Corp, was also present to see his uncle, Colonel M. C. Kennedy. He is the son of Mr. and Mrs. Russell Stevenson, of Schenectady, NY, and if he ain't got the sportiest, neatest little moustache you ever saw. It is a beaut. He looks fine. He told me that it is as easy to fly an airship, as it is to run an auto. He has some dandy black fur coat. He has driven some of the airships that have been captured from the Germans. Says the ones they captured before the war were all very good ones, well put up. I mean before the Armistice was signed, they were good ones.

But the ones that Germany is turning in now are not in such good shape, and Germany is not complying with the terms of the Armistice.

The colonel told him, "My boy, you will find it hard to make a silk purse out of a sow's ear."

He has no idea how soon he will be returned to the States, as they must try out all the German planes first. They are being turned over to the Allies.

Major Franklin ordered breakfast in the room and among other things he ordered was jam. The colonel said, "If it is strawberry jam, I don't care for any." Major said, "Captain T. B. and I have to eat as well as you, we will get through it." So the colonel said, "All right, sir."

Captain T. B. K. seemed to have a large interest in some sugar mine, as none in London saw any domino sugar for months, but he has a nice supply on hand and furnished the party with sugar, much to the satisfaction of all—me, too, cause the colonel handed me some over.

Captain T. B. K. then took the room by storm by going to the telephone and calling the starter and ordering an auto in French and believe me, he rattled it off. The colonel and the major told him he did well, and I could not help but say "Well done."

I wanted to get more information from both Captain T. B. K. and First Lieutenant Alex Stevenson, but the colonel was moving so fast and the questions he was asking were so deep I could not get what I was after. I had hoped to see them later, but did not get the chance. I was sure Lieutenant Stevenson had more up his sleeve as to the flying over the German borders.

By telephone, I was then to see Lieutenant George H. Stewart, who had engaged a room for me, and see where I was at for the night, for I intended to run all over Paris.

I found him at 246 St. Germain Blvd., and he fixed me up all right. He is the son of Mr. George H. Stewart, better known as the William Penn of Pennsylvania, in that he owns more land than any other man I know of in the dear old state.

He hails from Shippensburg, Pennsylvania, in the Cumberland Valley. After talking to me of the home folks, he puts me in charge of one of his soldiers. He is in charge of the lost baggage bureau and he has made good. He has gotten the baggage business now down to a good system, and it seemed that soldiers travelling were getting like women, always losing something—bed rolls, blankets, suit cases, cots, well they just had to lose something. He had gotten that all down in good shape and while I was in the office three soldiers came in hunting baggage they had lost, and it was found there, and they felt very much better, as they never expected to ever see it again.

Well, this little soldier's name was "Holland," and he and I started out. We saw the "La Grande Hone." I call it the ferris wheel. It is some wheel. Do not remember how high the man said it was, but it is up there some. I did not go up as it might go wrong when I was up there.

Went from there to La Tour Eiffel. I told him that was the first thing I wanted to see, as I had read of that for years. Well, I saw it. My thought was that it was closed, on the order of the Singer Building, in New York; but I find it is open and is a wireless station. You are not allowed inside now but you can get very close to it and can look it over very closely.

There is a beautiful park in front of it and the surroundings are very nice. I find that all through these cities they have many parks and they make things look very nice.

The Seine River passes between the Eiffel Tower and the Trocadero, a large hall similar to the Royal Albert Hall in London. The gardens around it are simply grand.

We then went to Notre Dame Church. That is one of the finest churches in Paris—in fact, one of the best in France.

It is sort of on an island, as the canal passes it on one side and about a block away the Seine River runs along, which forms a sort of an island. They were just taking the sand bags down from the front of it, which were put there to protect it from air raids.

It is a very beautiful church, with many handsome windows and the architectural work is handsome. By this time you will recognize that I have seen some churches, and I do not think I am capable of saying how it compares with others. It is very nice, but I think it is just a little better than we have in Chambersburg.

The canal passes right through the city and it is very nice. It branches off the Seine River way up in the city and it makes a very pretty picture to stand and see the canal boats and the barges being pulled down the river.

I was also in a place where Napoleon's Tomb is located and where, in the nearby open court, that great German aeroplane flier, Gunemier Zeppelin is on exhibition. However, I cannot recall the name.

In La Place de la Concorde there are two statues.

From the time Germany took Alsace and Lorraine, they always kept wreaths on these statues, but when the war was won they removed the wreaths. There is also a block there where they have cut off the heads of a few hundred people—so, all the sins are not committed on this side of the pond.

The traffic in Paris is to the right while in England it is to the left.

The Triumphal Arch has been closed to marching ever since Napoleon lost his battle at Waterloo. However, now that battle has been won by the French, it will be opened when the Peace Meeting is held in Paris within the next few days, in which President Wilson thinks he must be there to say what is what, and Mrs. Wilson thinks she also should be present. The parade will march through this Arch.

There are many buildings that show the effect of the bombing. Pieces torn out of the buildings. As soon as a bomb fell it was covered up as soon as possible and no one was allowed to talk about it or to say where it fell—that would give the Germans information of the amount of damage done.

French and American troops celebrate the Armistice near the Arc de Triomphe in Paris on November 13, 1918. The original caption read, "The allies whooping it . . . up." Courtesy of the National Archives and Record Administration, College Park, Maryland, 30090[990V8]

I find all the buildings decorated for the president when he arrives on the scene. Paris is a wonderful place for dogs. The women work very hard, pulling wagons or carts, and some of them have a large dog with a sort of a collar and they help pull the load.

I went to the Meurice Hotel at six in the evening. I was really tired. I have no idea of the number of miles I walked that day. On my way out, I saw Brigadier General W. W. Atterbury. He spoke to me and asked me how I liked Paris. I told him what Mr. Fahnestock and Mr. George Dallas Dixon said of him, and Colonel Kennedy, that they saw ten years ahead of other people when they went over here to help win this war. If they could get over now, they would willingly come. He laughed at it and told me to be sure not to get lost. He looked the very picture of health and I bid him good-bye and went out to see that great Fifth Avenue of Paris.

The Panorama du Louvre is a large and very handsome building. It was from this place that the great picture "Mona Lisa" was stolen.

Captured German war materiel was displayed on the Place de la Concorde in Paris just before the Armistice. A partially inflated German observation balloon is what remains of the German fleet of airships. Courtesy of the National Archives and Records Administration, College Park, Maryland, 30099[1064V8]

An unidentified African American soldier poses for a studio portrait in France. Behind him the flags of the United States and France hang prominently to represent the Allied forces. Such images were often taken by African American soldiers to record their service in France during the war. The photo postcards were also testimonies or evidence of how the experience abroad transformed their view of themselves in the world. Author's collection

We left Paris at 11:45 a.m. on Sunday in a five-passenger Vauxhall auto, for Montreuil, on the NE coast of France, on the English Channel.

Everything seemed to be going all right. We had what we thought was a good chauffeur and the car was making good time. We had dinner at Beauvais at 1:50 p.m. and I think we had covered about fifty miles up until about that time.

Beauvais is a small town with one of those little roadside houses, with a long table in the sitting room. The food was just fairly well cooked and there was none too much served. They had no trouble having nerve enough to charge me thirteen francs and some fifty-cent for the chauffeur and my dinner.

Well, the chauffeur got real chummy with me and you can rest assured I was plying him with all kinds of questions of the things we would likely

Royal A. Christian saw England and the battlefields of France from a car similar to this six-cylinder, forty-five-horsepower Vauxhall. An important contribution to the war effort, the British-manufactured Vauxhall was a fast and safe form of transportation. The four-cylinder version with its solid chassis, durable engine, and bicycle-style tires was capable of transporting four or five passengers at around sixty miles per hour. Courtesy of the National Archives and Records Administration, College Park, Maryland, 51328[129F9]

see on the route we were taking. Montreuil was about one hundred and twenty miles from Paris. They call miles over there kilometers.

About 3:00 p.m. this Vauxhall motorcar got cross and all the mean ugly things an auto can do it did. We coaxed and begged, but nothing doing. Finally, Major Franklin suggested a few things, which were tried but it went for about five or ten miles then she would spit and bark again. This continued until we reached Amiens, which we were anxious to see before dark. We were due there about 4:00 p.m. and we actually arrived at 5:15 p.m. too dark to see a thing.

Well, colonel and the major went into the Town Major's and got the GHQ on the phone and told them their troubles, and the chauffer was working his head off trying to doctor up what he called the "Carburater." I will never forget that name. I had coaxed everybody I knew at home to teach me something about an auto, but no one would do so, so I was of no assistance in this trying time.

While they were still talking, I wanted some cards of the City of Amiens and you can imagine the colonel and the major were not interested. Because of this, in the best of humor, I was sort of afraid to stray away. I listened to the conversation at the door and when I felt they were far enough that they would not stop within the next few minutes, I flew to the store and bought a book of the town, and was back all right in good time.

They talked to the chauffeur and it was decided to try to make the Third Army Headquarters, which was at Flixecourt. He said he would have no trouble in getting another car there, and off we started. The car ran for a few miles, and then it started the western tricks of barking, bucking and kicking. The chauffeur told me to pump. Well I pumped until I thought my arm would fall off, but as long as I pumped the car ran pretty fair and I felt at last I was of some direct benefit. He told me we only had about seven miles to go. I am sure I pumped her for fifty miles the way I felt over it.

Just as we were going up a large hill to the Third Army Headquarters, she died on the hill. The party got out and went to the office and shortly after they had everybody on their toes. We got a new car and chauffeur. The officers went into the Club and got something to eat. I got a fist full of sandwiches and a bottle of ginger ale, which was no trouble for me to get away with. It was then 10:00 p.m.

I was very sorry for the chauffeur, as he wanted to continue the trip. But, I was very glad the chauffeur was not Erwin Zimmermann of the states, whom I know.

The car we got here was all right and we went straight to Montreuil, arriving there at 11:25 p.m.

At Amiens, while we were lamenting over our troubles, some soldiers stole the general's Vauxhall Motor that was standing just about twenty-five feet from where our chauffeur and his friend were trying to fix the car.

We passed over the Somme River about three times between Amiens and Flixecourt.

Well, as it was late, I saw that the colonel and major were comfortable in their beds and I then turned in.

I got up the following morning pretty early to look over the place. It is a very large house and sets way up on a knoll, and I find the place belonged to Count De Premont and is called Chateau. It has been at one time a very beautiful place, but evidently, as the other chauffeur that had taken us out said, he had not much money and did not keep up the repairs on the place that it needed. There was quite a large amount of land to it and also quite a nice polo ground connected thereto, but the interior of the place needed many repairs. It is just about twelve miles from the English Channel and it is said on a clear day you can see the channel.

This GHQ is the British Headquarters and they have a large force of clerks on duty, and a number of regulation army huts for the soldiers and the women clerks. The place looks more like a hotel than a house, as is the rule in such places. The owner of the place had a crown erected over the top in front of his stable, which was a very large one.

We left there at 10:10 a.m. on Monday for the Hindenburg Line in another Vauxhall car belonging to General Cruikshank of the GHQ Staff.

Colonel Kennedy, Major Franklin, and Major Garden as guide, and your humble servant.

This car was running fine and it was a beautiful day for just such a trip. We pass Beaurainville and I see possibly about two hundred German prisoners working at a camp. The only thing not right about it was that they were not working them hard enough. The roads were simply fine and the chauffeur says they were built by Napoleon. They could hardly have been better for an auto. We pass through St. Pol. It is a sort of factory town. The idea seems to be in these countries over here to have a house set back in the yard and all through the country districts that is the case. Now just imagine a house setting back in the yard with a barnyard in front of it—that is just what you see. Of all the dirt and mud in the barnyard, you pass through there to the house. And then nearly every farm has a large pond of black looking water—looks simply filthy. It is not fit to drink for the occupants of the house or the stock, but they claim it keeps disease away. Each farm has one and from the way the people look they live to be very old. I saw some that surely from appearance they must have seen the one hundred mark long ago. At Neufchatel, I saw a young girl leading three cows with a rope with as much ease as you see a lady in London leading a pet dog.

There are practically no fences along any of the fields in France, and the soil looks good and they seem to be very well farmed. No ground seems to be going to waste. Turnips are raised here by the tons. I have never seen so many as I have here. They are fed to the stock. Women certainly do their share of the work. Carts are used, more so than wagons, and they are of the high-wheel variety. The load that is put on them is as much as could be put on any wagon.

We arrived at Arras at 12:15 p.m. and the party took lunch at the Saskatoon Club. I looked the town over quickly around the club and a few streets. It has certainly been badly used up. The Cathedral is a complete wreck. It is said to have been a very pretty one. It is nothing but a pile of rock now. I understand the Germans did not fly over Arras and bomb it, but bombed it from a distance. Many houses you will see are nothing more than walls standing. Some of them are entirely flat.

I walked into the Cathedral and stood and looked at what was the altar. The wall had caved in and broken the head of one of the statues, and pieces of the roof looked like they might come down any minute.

We leave Arras at 1:10 a.m. for farther up the line near Bethune. All along we see trenches. They are about five feet or six feet deep. At Allen, we saw the reserve trenches of the Allies. They are near the road and were not needed. Now that we are in the real fighting lines and dugouts and trenches, shell holes are plentiful. I would sure like to go over the field for a souvenir, but it is said one must be careful what you pick up as you might get hold of a "Booby trap" and get shot, as the Germans had many of them placed over the battlegrounds.

We then passed along where there were at one time villages and now there was not a piece of wall standing over three feet high—so great was the destruction. In many places I saw women and men standing by a little fire in what was their homes. There was absolutely nothing but

Both during and after the war, African American soldiers provided the labor to move materials to the front, repair battle-torn fields, and dig graves. Here, African American stevedores at La Havre load barges with rolls of tarpaper in February 1919. Courtesy of the National Archives and Records Administration, College Park, Maryland, 51379[2104F9]

a pile of debris. They were holding on to that. Some would be digging into the dirt to see what they could find.

Now, the dugouts are all along the roads and they are about four feet wide and a man won't need to bend over very much to get into one. The German ones are made out of concrete and you also see many concrete bases where the Germans fired their guns. You could see many places where shell holes were torn up for some long distance in the ground.

Many Chinese worked on the roads. They were kept up in good shape to help carry the provisions to the front line trenches.

It would be a good turn for the Red Cross women over here to go among the farmers and tell them to do away with the barn yards in front of their houses. Most of the women and girls in the fields wear wooden shoes. Near Lillers, I saw a fine large ox hitched to a plow, doing his bit.

The auto drivers over here seem to try and see how close they can drive to a person or team without hitting them and, not how far they

First Lieutenant Robert Conway Allen of the 372nd Infantry Regiment was honored with the French Croix de Guerre with Bronze Star for valor during the Meuse-Argonne offensive. Similar to the 369th, the 372nd regiment was absorbed into the French Army's 157th infantry, also known as the Red Hand Division. From June to October 1918, the 372nd took part in some of the most brutal fighting of the war. Author's collection can keep away. It would be hard for a nervous woman to ride in the cars over here. They seem to delight in just brushing anything they pass. The driver we had on this trip turns corners that I would be afraid to turn with a wheelbarrow, much less a car. In the carts they drive, they often have two horses. Some have one horse in the shaft and two in front. At Abbeville, I saw one with three horses in front and one in the shaft. Many of the coalmines have been put out of business by the Germans. Along the battleground you can see a little plot of say twenty-five or thirty feet. It is a graveyard. They are well filled up and a stake pushed in at the head painted white, with a sort of a rosette of Red, White, and Blue on the cross of the stake.

The roads used by the Allies were all camouflaged with a sort of chicken wire wound with a sort of green cloth that hung along the side of the road that would be seen by the Germans. In some places they were shielded with a sort of gunnysack.

The huts were about eight or ten feet high and had a sheet of iron on the tops and frame wood on the sides. Most were lined inside with pasteboard. They were about forty to forty-five feet long and would hold a good many men. Many of the people driving with their teams of horses carry their guns with them daily. Almost as if they expected to run across some Germans.

I saw several men out hunting on Sunday. I guess the better the day, the better the deed with them.

At Vimy Ridge, I could not stand the temptations any longer so I went over into the field and I found four packs of shells that have not been exploded yet. They were right under a small bunch of weeds. Evidently, placed there by some soldier. I also found the top of a shell. These I will carry back to the States. I gave one to Major Franklin and the other to M. C. Kennedy Jr., and the other two I will hold. Now each rack had five shells in them, making twenty shells in all.

At the place called Souchet the damage was equally as bad as in the Lens district. It was in the Vimy Ridge that the Canadians lost so heavily. Trees that were healthy, and large ones at that, were cut off by the shellfire to stumps. They were many times shot through and not a leaf or sign of life any place among them.

In all, we covered about one hundred and seventy miles over that wonderful battleground, and a fellow could talk for years and never get it all told. At Etaples, they have the largest cemetery in France connected with the war. It is very large and certainly must have thousands of soldiers in it. One of the hospitals was hit and destroyed by a bomb. The chauffeur showed me as we were passing through where it stood. At many places, we saw large crowds of German soldiers going or coming from work, and at no place did I pity them for a minute.

In going over the battleground, I would surely have shed no tears if that car had given us some trouble. I saw many things that would have been fine souvenirs. I saw one very large shell that had been exploded. I can just imagine how that would have looked polished up. And there was one large dugout near what was one time a coalmine, now ruined. It was a large concrete dugout and I think I saw the top of a helmet. Well, I was so worried I could hardly hold myself in the auto. If only I could have gotten out for a few minutes, I would have had that auto loaded with relics.

The trenches do not run straight but sort of zig-zag, the same sort of way as the vessels run to keep from the submarine shots. What they call going over the top, is coming out over the top of your trench and going after the other fellow.

Some of the trenches we saw were very dry and some had water in them. There certainly would not be much protection for the soldier in the huts if a bomb were to fall on them.

At the Cathedral in Arras, there is a sign telling you not to touch anything and that they intend to keep the Cathedral as it is and not rebuild there on that spot. It is a relic of the war, by order of the French government.

It was in July that the American Forces first went through the Hindenburg Line with the Australians. I get it from someone in line there, that there had been an understanding between the French and the Germans that each side would not fire on each other when they were watering their horses.

So, when the American boys, full of pep, got into the fracas, they saw the Germans going down to water their horses, they cut loose and nearly wiped out the whole bunch of Germans. The French went after the Americans for doing that and the Americans told the French, they did not come over here to play with the damned war—they came over here to win and end the damned thing right off. From that day on, the Germans were being cut down right and left.

We arrived back at Montreuil, safe after seeing what many dollars will later be spent to see.

We sail from Boulogne at 9:30 a.m. Tuesday for London, via Folkestone. At the station there was some trouble with my passport.

Those things always made me feel bad. I sort of felt I was some trouble to the officers, but it was no fault of mine. There is no possible way for me to explain to you what it is to travel during these war times and the red tape that is necessary.

The officer told Major Franklin that there was no use in trying to talk about it, that my passport was not "vised" and I could not get on that boat and that there was no use in talking any more about it.

There was both a British and an American officer present. Well this same Major W. S. Franklin that I have told was in the A class, he never swore in his life and never takes a drop to stimulate the body, but he did tell that officer and only as a son of Harvard can tell, that he was an American officer and that I was employed by the American Army and that I have got to go on that boat with them, and at the last I saw the fellow's knees begin to wobble together. The both looked at him and Roy went aboard the ship. They finally said, how will you get him off on the other side. The major said, "Leave that to me."

The channel was very rough—very, very bad. There were over 1400 people on the ship—many soldiers, too. I thought once that I might get sick, but again I thought I should be a better sailor and forget about that after Major Franklin pulling me through that way. So I walked around to see what was doing. I never saw so many people sick in my life. Men and women, poor things, they were in some bad way. They looked all groggy out of the eyes and very pale. The odor was not of the best along about that time either.

But the colonel and the major had a very nice stateroom and were very comfortable.

I want to say here that I will never forget Major W. S. Franklin. I thought all the real good ones came from Princeton, but I must admit that Harvard turned out a star when he came through.

When we docked I looked for more trouble—thought that the person on the France side, not being equal to the emergency, might phone over some trouble for us on the England side, but when my turn came, and I was among the first to go before the customs people, the major just looked down on him and explained and the official said, "Go ahead." You should have seen me move.

On the train from there to Victoria Station and the trip is over. That is all that I can now recall of it. Trust it will be of some interest.

The chauffeur is going to send me a map and when I get tracing over that more will come into my noodle.

Things are commencing to happen now and it is necessary for me to write at night to keep up with some of the things I am seeing. I saw by the papers that a U-boat would be in the city here for a few weeks, or days, and I feared it would get away before I got back from the trip.

It was slated to go on the 12th, so as soon as I got back, instead of going to lunch the following day, I flew up to Westminster to see this boat.

It is about one hundred and seventy-five feet long and about twenty-five feet wide, and is marked UB 65. She is an ugly looking critter and has six mine nests on the deck. Now these mine nests are a long funnel shaped hole that is partly filled with water. Two mines will float in each one of those nests, and when the crew wants to use them, they have a way of forcing them to the top of the deck with air, and then they roll it off at the place they want to mine. The nests are about three feet in circumference and on the forward end of the boat, right under the gun. The boat carried a three-inch gun and is fitted out with wireless, which it can operate from the coning tower.

Now, right in front of the coning tower is a large plate of iron about four feet wide. By lifting and looking down in there you will see a very strong light. This is fitted out with wireless outfit. This is used in case the submarine is submerged and for some reason cannot raise. This lid is forced open and it being equipped with wireless also, the crew would be able to communicate with any vessel and receive assistance. The light is so strong that it will show even though the submarine is under water many feet. I do not remember the exact distance that was said. The light is covered with very heavy strong glass and these lids that I speak of are all air and watertight. They have a heavy rubber ring around the lids.

But the main thing that attracted my attention was the periscope. I have been told so many things about the size of the periscope that I had it figured about four or five feet wide.

The periscope runs from the coning tower and at the base it is about six or eight inches in circumference and it is sixteen feet long and it tapers down until at the top it is not more than three or possibly four inches. So that gives you a rough idea of how far in the water the submarine will be when he fires his torpedo. The periscope must be above the water for him to gauge for his shot. The gun is about six feet in front of the coning tower and when they submerge the boat, they put a watertight cap on the muzzle of the gun. The water does not affect the other part of the gun. They aim to have a mine float about four feet under the water. This boat carries eight torpedoes. The tubes are on the side and when the torpedoes are put in they are charged with compressed air, so that the minute they are released they are off on their deadly errand.

Now, over the tanks that the mines are carried in when the boat is submerged, they have an iron grate that prevents the mines from floating out. When they want it out, they force water into the tank or nest to bring the mine to the top or level of the boat. There is a hook on it. A rope is run through that and the same fastened on to a cable, which runs over the top of the boat and the mine is swung from this cable into the water, and when they get it at the place they want it, it is cut loose from the cable and floats with a sort of weight they put on it. The boat is submerged by filling large tanks under the boat with water. And when they want to rise, the water is forced out by compressed air.

It cost 1 shilling to go on the sub and you were not allowed to go down into the vessel—only allowed on deck. I asked the sailor that I got this information from why you could not go down in the vessel and he said that there might be some German sympathizers that might do some damage. I told him, I was no German sympathizer and I would not do any harm. He said he did not believe I was in sympathy with Germany, but while he was sorry, he could not permit me to go down.

He explained to me something about the submarine. When the vessel is submerged the weight of the water on the vessel is so much that it is necessary to use a larger amount of horse-power to empty the tanks than the weight of the water on the vessel. Something like that. I cannot get that down right, so I will let it alone. That was too deep for me to understand.

I asked him if that vessel could cross the Atlantic. He said it could with ease. I also asked him how long did it take for a sub to go down or come up. He said he would not like to say. I do not know whether there was a secret to it and whether they cannot all be operated alike. As there were many other people on board at the time, I did not just like to ask all the questions, but it really did seem that those present were interested in what I did ask.

On Wednesday evening, Colonel Kennedy, with Captain F. C. Covell of the British Army, attended a boxing match at the Royal Albert Hall, but as yet he has not expressed himself along that line. Captain Covell is one of the officers that saved me in the harbor at Liverpool, and I will always remember him. Someday, he will come over to the States when things are properly straightened out here.

Sunday, December 15th, things are now drawing to a close for our party on this side of the pond.

Major W. S. Franklin received orders yesterday to go to Tours, France, for duty. Colonel Kennedy received a phone message, just a few minutes ago, from Tours, France, that his orders releasing him are on the way.

So you can see the dope is that we will sail on the *Mauretania*, which I understand will pull from Southampton about the 20th. That means that we will go from there to Brest, France, and from there to the United States. A better world than this.

Colonel Kennedy will give a farewell dinner at 14 Great Cumberland Place tomorrow, Monday evening, in honor of Major Walter S. Franklin, who has been his right-hand man during his stay in England. They have surely been very close to each other and have become almost inseparable. No one will miss the major more than I. He took great pains with me and I have learned many things from him.

I hope he will soon be returned to the States and that we will have the pleasure of looking after him in a real country.

Both the colonel and the major said when they were going to take me along with them to France, because I was not a good one on speaking French, they had better tag me, or some of the French authorities might pick me up as one of their subjects and ship me to Algeria, or some other place.

Lieutenant Houser and Sergeant Smith had one of those real swell dances last night. It was a private affair and the ladies, I understand, were masked. The costumes were simply grand. Smith has spent most of the morning trying to describe to me how well his friend looked. I wonder how the Brooklyn lady would admire the costume.

On Monday evening, Colonel M. C. Kennedy gave a dinner in honor of Major W. S. Franklin, who left this morning to take up his new duties at Tours, France. It was a very pleasant evening but it seemed to lack the usual pep that the dinners had always been blessed with. Everyone was very sorry to see Major Franklin depart from this base.

It is true that the best of friends must part, but when the time comes one cannot help but feel the parting.

Those present: Colonel M. C. Kennedy, Major E. S. Neilson, Captain L. G. Miller, Lieutenant C. T. Mackenson, Lewis B. McBride.

That takes out one more link in the party of the mess. The largest turkey that could be found was used for this occasion, and we had it well filled with oysters. The major is very fond of his eats and we spared no pains to see that he had all the dishes he liked.

And now the colonel has received orders that he can be released, and he at once engaged passage on the *Mauretania* which sails from Southampton, England, on Friday, December 20th. This will close my very interesting doings in London.

There is only one thing that I am worried about now, and that is the customs house and this book. When I hit New York and get through without showing the customs officials what I have in this book, then I will be one happy boy.

I hardly think there is anything in this book that would be objectionable, but they might want to read it first, and I do not want it that way. But, I do want the colonel's mother to see it and then his family.

I told the major when I said good-bye to him this morning that I would surely miss him when it comes to getting on and off the ship.

I will start to pack trunks tonight. The following cable was sent this morning.

Kennedy, Chambersburg, Pa.
Arrive New York *Mauretania* about thirty-first.

KENNEDY.

Thursday, December 19th, I packed the cold storage trunk—that is a trunk that you will not need to go into during the trip overseas—on Friday and Saturday I fixed up the others. On Sunday morning at 6:45 a.m., the autos called at 14 Great Cumberland Place and we left for Waterloo Station. As we drove off, we were bidding good-bye to London.

We arrived at the Waterloo Train Station at 7:55 a.m. for an 8:20 a.m. departure. After checking the baggage, the colonel did the honors with the baggage man. And, by the way, I must say if you don't look after him, you will likely get left, cause they are after the tip always. We left on the 8:20 a.m. train—getting away at 8:27 a.m., a few minutes late. The train was a fair one, making all stops en route to Southampton.

The train continued to get late all the way and we were due [at] Southampton at 10:10 a.m. but finally arrived there at 1:10 p.m. Well, better late than never.

Lieutenant John T. Henry, our embarkation officer, was on the job. He met the party with his staff, and after getting the information from the party he said to me, "Let me see your passports." I soon produced

The two men identified in this image, First Lieutenant J. T. Henry, US Army, embarkation officer (right) with Brigadier General A. G. Balfour, CB, British embarkation commander (left), represent only part of the narrative in this photograph. In the background, soldiers carry wooden crates up the gangplank to the ship docked at Southampton, England. These black men served as the visible but also invisible labor responsible for loading and unloading supply ships both during and after the war. Courtesy of the National Archives and Record Administration, College Park, Maryland, 45774[2113T8]

them to him. "Now," he said, "You are all right. I must have you see the alien officer as soon as he comes. Your room is B-84." Well, I began to feel fairly well. After seeing a great many wounded soldiers getting aboard, I saw a man with a blue uniform and cap on. I looked at Lieutenant Henry and he gave me the nod. I went near him and I heard him say that he wanted a desk. He said, "I have sent for a man." The alien officer said, "One of those cots turned upside down will answer all right."

I went to the cot, turned it upside down and made the desk. The alien officer stood right beside me and said, "That was fine." All the time I was telling him that I was with Colonel Kennedy, who was aboard the ship and was telling him of my passports that he was to look at. When I was finished with the desk, he said, "Now, let me see your passports," which made me the first one he looked at. I produced them in double-quick time. He looked them over and said, "You are all right." But to my sorrow, he asked for my ration book and also my identity book. I wanted to keep both of them as souvenirs. Well, I handed them over and he said I could go aboard, and I was not long getting up the gangplank.

After getting up on the vessel and seeing the purser, I found that the number given me by Lieutenant Henry was O.K. and you can imagine my surprise when I found it was a stateroom on B deck of the real ship *Mauretania.*

During all the time I was packing up at the house, the colonel would say to me, "Now Roy, see if you can get everything in the trunks, but don't put the cook stove in." The thought occurred to me that if I got everything in I would be satisfied to leave the cook-stove out. He sure will joke with you. He hands it out so quick at times that if you don't think fast you won't see that he is putting one over on you.

I went aboard the ship at about 2:25 p.m. and I took a sort of look over England, and I said good-bye. And, I did not intend to get off unless something went wrong. Everything was passing off all right and everybody that was aboard at that time was happy.

With the purser and the colonel, I was shown to my stateroom. Now, be sure and get that "State-Room." Well, when I looked into that I just looked at the colonel and thought you sure stepped some that time. He then told the head waiter that I was his man and that he wanted me taken care of, and the head waiter commenced bowing at once, and Roy was all fizzed up with this wonderful state-room in my head. You know I was "IT" now, and the head waiter was looking me over and telling the rest of his crew to be careful of me, that I was somebody. And, I was, too.

Well, after everything was all straightened out and everybody was seemingly fixed for the trip, they began to put on the wounded and there were about three hundred cases of them, some walking cases, some on cots. Each soldier walking or on cots was given by the Red Cross a silk flag, pack of cigarettes, two bars of chocolate, and a silk khaki handkerchief.

Well, after looking over the ship and seeing that all was happy and that the ship looked like she could carry the load, I thought it was time to get some information on the real make-up of the ship and what she could do.

Monday, December 23rd, I got up about 6:30 a.m. and the weather looked as if it was going to be a fair day. There was nothing startling going on until all at once at 8:00 a.m. the band of the ship *Louisville* of the USA that was lying at the dock, played at colors the "Star Spangled Banner" and then "God Save The King." People here in America might guess how a fellow feels when these stunts are coming off, but none will ever know that have never gone through it. Again, at 1:15 p.m. the same band came back on the customs house platform and in honor of Captain Cone of the Navy, they played until the ship pulled from the dock at 2:05 p.m. the crowds cheering and yelling themselves hoarse. As the tugs pulled this real ship away from the dock the band played "My Old Kentucky Home" and "Star Spangled Banner" again. Well, honestly, if you saw the kaiser at that time, you would not hesitate one moment to kill him. Captain Cone came out on the deck and waved good-bye to them. I had known Captain Cone some, but on the way over I learned to know him better. I would certainly have liked to have been near him to hear his thoughts of the people—waving goodbye. He was the finest man to express himself I ever heard.

It rained some and the air was chilly. Many large hospitals are seen leaving England. With my little bed it reminds me of my stateroom on Car 41. After getting out in the Channel, we received a cable from Mr. T. B. Kennedy, assistant to president of the CVRR, that he would meet us at New York. This baby was certainly going some through the sea. There are two forts just out of Southampton that form a sort of gateway by which every ship going into England must pass, and one can readily realize that should a ship go through there otherwise, it will get its medicine. The baby pulled at 2:00 p.m. and she gets under way and we head for Brest, France, arriving there Tuesday morning at 7:15 a.m.

Tuesday, 24th: About 5:15 p.m., I see the lights from the lighthouses through the English Channel. They are very strong and we travel on the way down the English Channel to the harbor of Brest, France.

Arriving there at 7:15 a.m., we see the destroyers spinning through the waters and they, I think, make fifty miles an hour when they want to.

At 11:55 a.m. the troops began to gather. You see, after getting on the wounded at Southampton, we were to get aboard about five thousand troops at Brest, and there would have been some doing had not there been some going ahead.

Finally lighters *Rintintin, Kingfisher, Cubs, Fall River,* and *Nenette* came up with soldiers. They were packed so tight that they looked like flies. There was a Mr. P. D. Cravath, also, who engaged the adjoining stateroom to Colonel Kennedy. You can feel that I wanted to look him over—he was from New York City. He finally got aboard and I saw that he was a pretty warm looking member. He was about sixty-five or seventy years of age and had the, or I will say, one of the finest outfits of clothes for a man of that age I ever saw: Two pairs of trousers to each suit and two suits alike of each kind, even to Tuxedo and Dress Coat. Well, he certainly was a good dresser. I went up to him and delivered the message from the colonel and got in his good graces at once. I saw he fell for the services that the colonel had told me to render and I sure was "Johnny on the spot."

There was a long delay in the boat moving out after she got on her load, and the colonel told me if we had this ship up on the Conococheague we would get it started on time.

As there are possibly other persons that know any time important parties started for home they wanted to move, and they delight to go fast. I would not do a thing to make them wait one minute for a large price of money.

Well, the colonel had told me to do anything I could for Mr. Cravath. I fixed up two pairs of shoes for him and had hoped to do more before I reached New York. At 4:30 p.m., we started to sea. Captain Cone's bluejacket from the Naval Hospital went ashore and got left. Captain Cone, you will remember, was badly hurt when the ship *Leinster*, a mail ship, was hit by a German submarine near the Irish Coast. The first torpedo that hit it broke one leg and he tried to help the women, of whom there were many on the ship, to safety, when along came the second and broke the other leg in two places. He fell on deck and as the ship began to sink he rolled off the deck into the sea and then finding that he could not use his legs, that they were broke, he swam dog fashion and was drawn down with the vessel and he says how on earth he came to the top he does not know, but that is what he did.

Now, this bluejacket was to bathe Captain Cone's leg and dress him, and now that he was left, it was decided that Roy was to get that job. One thing you could book on—the only way Roy would get off that ship was to throw him off. I like to see every place that has any attraction but on a trip like this—no chances for me. I had served Captain Cone several times at Great Cumberland Place and knew him. He is one of those real men, nervy, full of pep, no fear in him. Nothing would have suited me better than to have seen him have a little chase with the kaiser's ships. He could beat any man cussing I ever heard, and he kept you laughing from the time you started to dress him until you left with the most witty sayings and jokes. When I would take his clothes off and put his pajamas on, the surgeon would work his foot. It seemed that some of the leaders in the foot were dead. When Dr. Lane would work a little rough, he would say, "Hell, Doc., hold on, you are rough as hell with that paw of mine tonight." Well Captain Twining and the whole party would laugh, and then Captain Cone would burst out and laugh with the rest.

After carefully tucking the colonel and the captain in their little beds, Mr. Cravath did not show up until 10:45 p.m. then I carefully laid him away. I looked at the soldiers—they were busy trimming up the boat with laurel and holly, and they had really nearly bought the candy man in the canteen out, as they bought, stood and ate it by the pounds.

It now being 1:10 a.m., I thought I had just about seen all of interest, so I turned in for the night.

Wednesday, December 25th: At 6:00 a.m. there was a strong wind and the sea was rough, throwing the spray far up on deck. The ship was making about eighteen knots. We passed two ships and I hear at breakfast they are going to start fire in her other boilers and that they are going to widen on her and let her step.

About 3:30 p.m. that afternoon, I was standing on the deck, listening to what the waves were saying. As the passengers were passing along exercising, Mr. Cravath walked up to me and said, "Roy, I want to introduce you to Mr. Morrow." He at once extended his hand to shake hands. I gave him that pleasant bow and Mr. Cravath said, "Roy has been the servant for Colonel Kennedy for many years and has kept the colonel looking very pretty and in good health, and now the colonel has added me to the list and Roy, in addition to his duties, looks after me." Mr. Morrow said that was fine. He asked me of my duties in London and you know he got it in full.

Mr. Cravath said, "He is a very handy servant and does his duties well." Well, you know if you have a servant working for you and his head is not entirely full of saw dust, it won't hurt to tell him some times that he does some things well. So that went down all right. They said a few other nice things and left. That night, I waited to take off Mr. Cravath's shoes. It was about 11:30 p.m. when he turned in and I was after more information on Mr. Morrow. I hardly knew how to go about it, but I finally got out and said, "Mr. Cravath, is Mr. Morrow from New York?" He said, "Oh, yes, that gentleman I introduced you to today was Mr. Dwight Morrow, one of the main members in the firm of J. Pierpont Morgan Co., New York, and he is a very able man." Well, I liked to fall over.

They served a very nice dinner this evening and it seems that this salt air keeps my appetite just about right. The plum pudding was real right. I don't know whether a minister would have gone against it or not, but it was sure right.

Many soldiers are getting sick on this trip but I think this ship is very smooth sailing. One soldier said to me the other day, "Did you get some of that good chicken at dinner?" "No, pal," he said, "it seems the least I put in my stomach the better off I am." The other fellow said, "Why it seems to me I cannot get enough in my little belly." It is a remarkable thing the make-up of some men.

And while the ship was sailing smoothly along, the colonel was in such a happy mood as the ship was heading you know toward "Ragged Edge." At about 4:00 p.m., I looked in on him, to see if he was riding comfortably when he, well, very kindly opened up that wallet. I always did think it was a fine pocket book, but on this date, well, it was great. One of those handsome bills was leafed off and Roy was right under it, you know. And was not that a fitting ending for Christmas Day on the high seas?

Thursday: At 6:20 a.m., she is sailing fine. It is not yet daylight. The members of the crew say she is making twenty-six knots. When I dressed the captain he said it was doing over eighteen knots and that she would dock Monday and unload Tuesday.

They have all the soldiers out on deck for inspection this morning. It lasted for three-quarters of an hour. Got very hazy at about 4:30 p.m. Everyone feared they would cut down the speed and no one wanted to see that. We have the 134th Infantry Band aboard and they give a concert on the B deck at 12:00 Noon and about 6:45 p.m.

It got very rough at night and we slowed down a bit—the sea beat real high over the decks.

They had exercises in the lounge and several speakers helped to make things lively for the officers, while the band touched up the air with that real rag stuff. While I was talking to some soldiers about the conditions at Brest, crossed-wires started a fire on the starboard side of the ship, right above the column I was leaning against. They sure are sore at the camp there. The crew was called and the fire was soon put out. I walked around to the other side while they put it out. You know with a large bunch of crazy soldiers, somebody might get bumped off.

The miles made per day is taken from 12:00 p.m. one day until 12:00 p.m. the next day. From 4:20 p.m. Tuesday until 12:00 Noon

Wednesday she did 317 miles. Thursday she did 544 miles, Friday she did 591, Saturday 559, Sunday 525, and docked Monday at 11:50 a.m. I had too much to think of then to look for the miles. I understand this is the last trip of this ship with soldiers. She goes into dry-dock and will get all her fine trimmings back that were removed to carry soldiers, and she will take her place in Trans-Atlantic service. I assure you I have no objection to what she does.

Friday: The sea today is as smooth as a piece of glass. The soldiers are on deck for drill and their exercise stunts at 10:00 a.m. They are very kind to their wounded and carry them out on deck so they might see the waves and get fresh air. You know, white folks are very funny about plenty of fresh air. We colored folks don't need so much, cause I was plugging up holes in my stateroom, but they have us skint in many ways and possibly they are right about the fresh air business.

They put on three hundred cases of wounded soldiers at Southampton—many with legs off; one poor fellow had both legs and one arm off and an eye out.

But with all their troubles they are a happy lot. They seem very cheerful. That is one thing a fellow likes about a man. He never complains. Women, you know, as soon as they get a pain, they yell murder and get mad at everybody and themselves in particular. While a real man, like Captain Cone, takes things easy and keeps happy.

Saturday: They all say they are glad it is over and are anxious to get to God's Country again, and the main question is, "When will she dock?"

The sea was a little rough and sort of handled the ship to suit its needs. I was not a bit pleased with its conduct, but I did not register any knock. Colonel Kennedy is going to give the captain of the ship a box of cigars, and I am rather anxious to carry them for, you know, the captain will have to answer me some things. I have them framed how to ask him. I have two life preservers in my room—and if one will save you, certainly two should do the trick.

Sunday: Sea is still a little rough but not so much as yesterday. On the bulletin board it says there will be Catholic services held in the Lounge at 10:30 a.m. on the A Deck. Captain Cone told me this morning that I was doing fine. I was bathing his leg, said he never missed the damned blue-jacket and said if they kept kicking the railroads around and colonel could not use me, I should come to him and he would give me a job on his ship. Well, you know when a ship goes down they say, "Where is it?" But when you meet with a mishap on the railroad they say, "Here he is even if he don't look quite the same." I thanked him for his offer, but I ain't letting any pictures pull me away. There are a whole lot of Kennedys and I am trying to make hay for all of them and it will take a whole lot to draw Roy away. In fact, that blooming stateroom makes me say, "For life I am with you."

Just as I handed the cigars to Captain Rostrum, in came some friends of his. Well, if you ever saw a sore messenger you should have had a peep at me just about that time. I had all kinds of questions to ask the captain and had been waiting all along to take the cigars to him. In handing over such a good brand I knew it would make him feel pretty good and he would say a few things. The best I could do was to back out, which I did but without very good thoughts of Mr. and Mrs. Butt for butting in.

At 8:30 a.m. Monday, December 30th, we pulled up the river past the Statue of Liberty. The tugs came alongside and finally worked us up to the dock at 11:30 a.m. I went off the ship at 11:50 a.m. at Pier 54, New York. I gave a sigh of relief to know I had once again placed my feet on American soil.

There is no need to try to describe to you readers how a fellow feels when he sees the good old USA after being over in England. With all the real people singing and the flying of flags, and all that sort of thing, one cannot help but be happy.

Along with the state-room steward, I carried the baggage (hand) off the ship and waited from that until 4:45 p.m. for the trunks to come out of the hold of the ship and then until 5:20 p.m. when I got a truck to take me with the baggage to the Pennsylvania Railroad Station. There, I checked the baggage and got the 6:04 p.m. train for Philadelphia, where I arrived at 8:35 p.m. The thoughts of being back in the dear old Keystone State made me feel entirely different.

I have had many trials in trying to remember dates and occurrences. You will find after being away so long *you* forget dates too. There were many things that after going to see them, they would make an interesting story. I could not get cards to explain them, and several times I became so disgusted that I stopped writing for days. Then again I found I was lacking a little in the head to explain some things I did see. I am positive I could have made this book three hundred pages as easy as what I have.

But I trust all that take the time to read it will not feel their time is all lost, and that they will here and there find some things that will be interesting to them.

So, with the feeling that I was one of them that had the nerve to go across and help put the kaiser out of the running, and with a trip in my head that I shall never forget, I am

Very truly yours

ROYAL A. CHRISTIAN,
Confidential Messenger
American Army Headquarters,
Belgrave Mansion Hotel,
London, England.

Compliments of

Royal A. Christian

Room 701
Broad Street Station
Philadelphia, Pa.

Christian provided cards similar to this one in copies of his book that he gave to family, friends, and acquaintances. Courtesy Stuart A. Rose Manuscript, Archives, and Rare Book Library, Emory University

INDEX